cash
in on conflict

professional and personal
success through partnering

AuthorHouse™
1663 Liberty Drive, Suite 200
Bloomington, IN 47403
www.authorhouse.com
Phone: 1-800-839-8640

AuthorHouse™ UK Ltd.
500 Avebury Boulevard
Central Milton Keynes, MK9 2BE
www.authorhouse.co.uk
Phone: 0800 1974150

First published by AuthorHouse 8/8/06.

ISBN: 1-4259-5611-4 (sc)

Printed in the United States of America and the United Kingdom.

This book is printed on acid-free paper.

cash
in on conflict

professional and personal
success through partnering

charlie irvine

www.cashinonconflict.com

What people say about **Cash in on Conflict** and **Charlie Irvine's** work

A thought-provoking and timely analysis of Partnering. Charlie Irvine provides ideas and examples of how people and organisations can partner for mutual success – as has certainly been the case with the British Council and its partnership with Charlie's organisation, Questions of Difference.
Sir David Green, Director General, British Council

This is a dynamic and enjoyable read, which reveals the models and practices of Partnering. Charlie's work is relevant to many of the challenges we have yet to overcome in organisations and gives you the opportunity to breathe more life into situations that are proving difficult. If your organisation is serious about paying attention to the quality of conversation and relationships that make up how organisations deliver performance, then you should read this book.
June Boyle, Group Organisational Development Director, BT

This is a genuine attempt to challenge all of us to adopt a Partnering ethos. Charlie Irvine has generously captured his thinking and approach in a way that is readily accessible. *Cash in on Conflict* disrupts the way we think about and work with differences, much in the way those of us who have worked with Charlie have been positively disrupted.
Julia Marton-Lefèvre, Rector, UN-affiliated University for Peace.

You will be catapulted into a new way of thinking that could just make an adventure out of your day at the office tomorrow. And you will be laughing as you go.
Scilla Elworthy, Founder of Peace Direct, Winner of the Niwano Peace Prize 2003, three times nominated for the Nobel Peace Prize and international author.

Charlie Irvine has an intuitive understanding of cognitive behaviour. His book helps us to use our thoughts and feelings positively in order to create effective strategic partnerships. You can open this book at random and find a gem on every page.
Professor Shirley Pearce, Vice Chancellor, Loughborough University

www.cashinonconflict.com

About the Author

Charlie Irvine is an unconventional thinker, dynamic speaker and leader who is a strategic business consultant, focusing on organisational development and change, leadership and strategic partnerships, conflict management and team dynamics.

Since 1996, he has been Founder and Managing Director of Questions of Difference Ltd (QoD), a UK-based business of thinkers, facilitators and leaders working with organisations ranging from ACAS to AstraZeneca, BT to the British Council, eBay to FT, Inland Revenue to Merseyside Police and Royal Bank of Scotland to the UK Cabinet Office.

As a world-class facilitator, working with large and often conflicting groups, Charlie describes himself as a social enabler, someone who gives people a powerful shock to their imagination and helps them get curious enough to follow their passions. He brings his highly focused business approach to Partnering, a word and a concept that sounds so familiar to many people, yet which demands a profoundly different attitude to dealing with the differences between people within and between organisations and communities.

In addition Charlie is the Chairman of Peace Direct, a charity that is committed to learning from, promoting and funding local peace keeping initiatives across the world.

Questions of Difference Limited

Questions of Difference (QoD) is a niche consultancy – a company of social revolutionaries, experimental entrepreneurs, international thinkers, speakers, facilitators, leaders and social enablers.

Founded by Charlie Irvine in 1996, QoD have worked with over 30,000 people across 24 countries. With clients ranging from small organisations to those in the FTSE 100, the basis of their business strategy is to partner with organisations in a way that builds internal capability and draws on the existing strengths.

QoD specialise in motivational public speaking; designing and facilitating conferences and large scale events; design and delivery of cultural change programmes; assisting complex partnerships to achieve their objectives; challenging strategic thinking to drive organisations forward; developing leadership skills; resolving disputes between individuals or groups and working with teams to increase performance levels.

With a core belief that 'everything is possible' when working with QoD you can expect to be inspired; laugh out loud; have a shock to your imagination; be challenged; hear great colourful stories – and receive an injection of common sense.

www.qod.co.uk

Acknowledging my partners

Of two things I am absolutely clear – for me to have my name on a book as author, others need to have been involved; and to produce a book that introduces the magic of Partnering, we would not be true to the ethos without Partnering with others to produce it.

Not so very long ago an increasing number of people were asking where the book was. Can you send me something to read? Where can I read more about Partnering? Have you got something I can give my boss, customer, supplier, team, wife, neighbour – cat?

As someone who is clear on the importance of understanding strengths, I was sure that writing was not one of mine. Then, one day, I came across Mark Griffiths – a wordsmith whose passion for language is matched only by his passion for learning. So, Mark, this book would not exist had it not been for your skill, craft, passion, sense of fun and incredible capacity to get me to read and write stuff that you then so beautifully make sense of. Your business could not have a more perfect name – Ideal Word captures what you and your partner Debbie produce.

Having found our wordsmith, the most obvious step was to work with the Questions of Difference team to make it happen. To Graeme, my colleague and mate, and Sara, my life partner and colleague, thank you for the playful times in the green kitchen, the editing and story telling, the patience and persistence in getting this done. To the other members of our team, Marianne and Anne, thank you for the proofing, diary management and stories you gave us that made the points come to life.

Once we had laughed a lot, re-written too many times, felt proud of what we had done and doubted we would ever get finished, we tucked our courage inside our audacity and sent our draft out to an international audience – from Nigeria to Ethiopia, Ghana to Scotland, South Africa to Wales, Oxford to London. Our unsuspecting team of academics, leaders, lawyers, activists, friends, publishers and, may we say it, successful authors, all reviewed our work and provided great feedback. So then we went away and re-wrote it all over again. Thanks, you guys!

With a powerful Partnering manuscript in our eager hands, we reminded ourselves that one of our main roles in life is to disrupt everyday assumptions and traditional expectations, where they could be different. All affirmatively, of course. So, in the interests of saving time and satisfying a waiting world, we decided to publish with Authorhouse, who have been to us everything we could have asked for, so I thank them. Now here's a Partnering concept for you: we research, write and design the book and hold the copyright; they trust our judgement on the content, print it and network it into major distributors. The costs are clear and up front and it all happens this year. Now, that's what I call affirmatively disruptive publishing!

Thanks also to the affirmatively disruptive design provided by Advantage Design Consultants. I have great expectations that our PR partner Platypus will now do their utmost to get this book into all the usual as well as the most unexpected places. Thanks for the work you will do.

I thank these and all my future Partners – my assumption is that this will be the first of who knows how many?

Charlie Irvine, London, 2006

Contents

Contents

Preface

My aim with this book is to provide you with an easy, amusing and engaging text that you can flip through in a few hours and then go back to later to remind yourself of the challenges that were presented, stories that made you chuckle, tools that were easy to use and apply as well as providing common sense approaches that you want to try in a new situation.

You will find each chapter is a combination of stories drawn from the last 10 years of my work in organisations and experiences of life, easy to use and apply common sense tools, plus some suggested actions that you can take now to Cash in on Conflict in your world.

Chapter 1 sets the overall context and provides a definition of Partnering. If you prefer to jump right in then do check out the spirits story before moving on to Chapter 2. In Chapter 2 I take a whistle-stop tour through making a case for freeing ourselves from models of Partnering – Partnering is too effective, dynamic and innovative to be limited by models! In this Chapter I also show that Partnering is a down the line, tough business ethos that delivers results quickly – ultimately pushing you beyond the limitations of win-win approaches.

Chapter 3 challenges you to think about the assumptions you hold and the language you use. It is a powerful wake up call for managers, leaders and businesses. I also introduce the TICing model in a way that can be instantly applied to help you make sense of the chaotic world of human communication. And do look out for the strawberries when you go there. As you meander into Chapter 4 be prepared to be jolted from the safe world of thinking that you cannot choose the assumptions you hold every minute of your day. In Chapter 4 I present seven Partnering assumptions, giving practical suggestions for how to instantly profit from applying them.

Chapter 5 focuses directly on conflict, providing a re definition of conflict and how to benefit from the disputes and differences you have. In addition to the six practical steps I have also included the wonderful but easy to apply MITS approach to resolving conflict. Finally if increasing customer satisfaction by 30% appeals to you, the StarFish approach to Cashing in on Conflict will reap dividends.

Chapter 6 goes into the world of questions and challenges you to start developing your own craft. I explore different types of questions including questions for understanding and intervention – and give you the Why question challenge! The last chapter continues our practical, get into action approach. Here I work with the day-to-day situations we all find ourselves in and provide quick actions, thoughts and challenges to help you achieve success through Partnering. From managing individuals, to making meetings effective to launching new Partnerships successfully – we get practical and take action.

Finally I pose a few questions that are aimed at taking you in new, familiar, exciting and vexing directions.

Have fun and enjoy the trip!

Charlie Irvine

Exploiting Difference

Partnering is the new
organisational DNA
for creating sustainable
success

Getting into the spirit of Partnering

If you're brave enough to cash in on conflict, you will have to take a radically different approach to the way you exploit – yes I mean exploit – the differences between people in your organisation, your community, your life. Even more, when you cash in on conflict and achieve success through Partnering, you will be exploiting the differences in you.

Partnering is profoundly familiar to us yet pushes us way beyond what we think is possible. Whoever you are, wherever you are, in whatever capacity you operate, you and your organisation or community will have to think yourselves fitter faster. The challenge and opportunity to cash in on conflict and achieve success through Partnering is everywhere.

When you think of the Great British Spirit, what comes to mind? The success of a small nation in becoming the first superpower of the modern world? What comes to the fore when you meet the Nigerian Attitude? A fierce determination to get on with life and take a great big bite out of it? Does the American Dream conjure up hope and possibility? How about the aspirations of Islam – for some of the poorest nations in the world to be treated with respect?

Perhaps none of these. All are assumptions – voluntary positions we can take and do take as individuals. When combined with the assumptions of others in our communities and cultures, these assumptions can resonate powerfully in the world.

As the recent momentum of good intentions slows down and people hesitate over a contribution to alleviate famine in Africa or provide shelter in Pakistan, or shrink in the face of bombers and constant security alerts, they begin to wonder how they can continue making a difference. British people are constrained by the culture of a backs-to-the-wall spirit, yet there are signs they want to break out and discover in themselves what made their country great.

People inside your organisation are crying out for practical ways to sustain this kind of thinking – to liberate themselves from that hopeless feeling that real change can never happen in one lifetime, never mind one financial quarter.

People value Community Spirit – and they notice when it is not present. They say that it is lost because of people's attitudes.

How often do we put a number of our social issues down to the loss of our old sense of community? What would it take for us to realise that we are the community, we are not lost, we can change it?

Adopting a Partnering ethos means acquiring an attitude and a spirit towards change that makes things possible between people in organisations and communities of all shapes and sizes – and makes things possible *because* of the differences rather than despite them.

One too many spirits!

I was sitting enjoying the hospitality of an airport lounge in Stockholm when my mobile phone rang with what turned out to be one of those commonplace yet bizarre requests for help. Essentially the person explained that she represented one of two organisations that were in conflict. What you might find surprising was that, although the conflict had been raging for close to 20 years and all the people who had started it were long gone, the people who now represented each organisation had remained absolutely loyal to the dispute.

One of the organisations was a public sector Local Authority responsible for funding voluntary organisations in their local area. The other was a voluntary organisation that provided care for people with learning difficulties. As we began to discuss the issues and what was required of me, I struggled to stop my mind wandering at the absurdity of the situation (perhaps it was the impact of the lounge rather than the story).

How do we get ourselves into these situations? This story is by no means unique. Perhaps you are thinking of a similar example yourself. People who are passionate about doing valuable work end up embroiled in painful and protracted disputes that rage unchecked like forest fires, long beyond the initial spark that lit the tinder. Now, nearly 20 years down the line, these two organisations were looking at a last-ditch attempt to resolve their issues before going to court.

As I was legging it down the stairs for my flight, trying not to sound like I hadn't partnered with my body for the last 20 years, I was told that the organisations had decided to invest in working with me for one day – if that didn't sort things out, then they were off to court. I assured the person that I would call the moment I landed in the UK and that I was certain we could sort something out.

As the plane took off and the passenger next to me banged on about the delays, poor service, lack of information, size of the seats, I began to think about the conversation I'd just had.

What brings people and organisations to subject themselves to this kind of environment for so many years? More importantly, what made them now believe that one day was going to resolve 20 years of negative conflict?

Slightly distracted, I also wondered what on earth had happened that day to my fellow passenger that he was so irate about the world. Having learnt more subtle ways of expressing displeasure since moving to the UK, I played the usual game of looking up into the distance, not particularly focusing on anything, then giving sideways glances, quickly looking away if there was any chance of him catching my eye. What I did notice was that the person behind me was starting to express her displeasure at our fellow passenger by pushing the back of his seat every time he sounded off about something. I could see that this was turning into an interesting flight – air rage was alive and well. How come this lot could not get over themselves and stop this playground behaviour?

As I started to turn the volume of my iPod up, I suddenly wondered what on earth made me think I could help these two organisations if I did nothing about the individual situation that was unfolding in front of me. I screwed my courage to the sticking point and, turning to my fellow flier, asked "Are you going somewhere nice?" He turned to face me, with a jaw slack with shock. Who was this tall stranger to be interfering in his personal world of rage? And so we began to chat. After a few conversations and tense moments I discovered a thing or two. My fellow passenger had also received a call as he was boarding the plane – his call was from a very distraught wife who was at the hospital where their daughter was in intensive care having attempted suicide. How many times, I thought, does this sort of thing need to happen to me before I learn to start engaging with someone using different assumptions?

On my return to London I began to prepare for my date with dispute by meeting with each group involved. I was astounded to discover the number of strategies and tactics they had employed to 'manage' their differences. I suspect that some of these will be very familiar to you – the filing cabinets were overflowing with letters, documents, memos and the minutes of endless meetings. I quickly saw that if I were to try and understand the 'facts' then I would be planning my retirement before I was finished. The amount of energy and passion that so many people had put into this conflict was incredible – and it was called a partnership. As I walked to the group meeting that morning I began to wonder how much the hospitality of the BA lounge had contributed to me taking on this job – they get nearly 20 years to have conflict and I get one day to work with them to resolve it. Hardly seemed fair, but then maybe 'fair' is overrated. And yet, when we actually addressed the situation, face to face, in direct conversation, progress was rapid. It was almost as though they were all desperate to sort this thing out, if only someone would give them permission to let it go.

What is it that makes people limit themselves by assuming that change takes a long time?

By the time we had finished our sandwiches at lunch, the group had moved forward and people were discussing their divorce – yes, divorce. It turned out that once we started to explore the assumptions everyone was holding, there was nothing stopping either organisation from re-defining the business relationship they had. By using the language of divorce they started to see that they could liberate themselves from their current ways of working and determine how to partner more effectively in the future.

Essentially, it took a few hours to get the people in the room to review their assumptions, see their differences as a significant resource and, most importantly, give themselves permission to take different decisions. Like responsible parents in our modern world, having agreed the terms of their divorce, both parties could then make their commitment to establish a different relationship that was in the best interests of the children. Divorce for these organisations did not mean a simple parting of the ways, never to meet again. It meant re-evaluating what sort of relationship they needed to have to deliver their responsibilities.

What had seemed so difficult for these organisations for so long did not turn out to be so difficult at all. I would say that – I describe myself as a serial optimist. Optimism is where I always begin – that mixture of hope, curiosity and passion, the building blocks of personal and collective transformation.

The need for Partnering

I know from my own working experience that Partnering means significantly upping your game by working with the reality that the differences between people in your organisation and life can be the greatest source of development for you and for them.

I have used the word Partnering precisely because it is not a new word for anyone. For me, the notion of 'a Partnering ethos' is a very, very conscious choice, because everyone who uses it draws on a multitude of experiences, good and bad. Yet, *as an organisational DNA*, Partnering is absolutely new.

To use the phrase 'cash in on conflict' is disturbing for some. Yet until organisations and the individuals within them develop the capacity to truly get the most from their conflicts and differences, hostilities, cynicism, mediocrity, inertia and boredom will continue to plague them and their desire for innovation, creativity and things to be different will not be satisfied.

What could be different?

Let's look around ourselves. Everywhere conflict and change, change and conflict. Name any situation of conflict you can think of – from riots in French cities, to insurgents in Iraq, to territorial disputes in Sudan, to striking rail workers in the UK, to unco-operative managers in business departments anywhere in the world. News bulletins feature war and violence, disagreement and rancour, cultural disputes and generational turbulence. So much difference of opinion, attitude, culture, belief. The more connected the world becomes, the more striking the differences between us. People are taking action and behaving in ways that others find distressing and unacceptable, because they feel they have not been heard in ways that are acceptable. How sustainable is the direction we are all taking our world in?

Every day, society's decision-makers – from politicians to community leaders to marketers and business people large and small – are encountering such fulminating questions that seem too hot to handle.

People in all sorts of organisations constantly talk, discuss and sometimes meet (in the corridors) about wanting things to be different, wanting the changes they desire to be sustainable, needing to make better sense of the increasingly complex environments they operate in, groping for answers that explain the actions of others. They keep getting stuck because making a difference means taking on difference.

So many of us strive for and have a vision that things must, can and should be different – a world in constant destructive conflict and fear of each other is unsustainable – and we constantly struggle with how to make this happen.

People talk about how to make a difference, then they struggle how to think about what could be different, then they find it difficult to make their actions link up to their thinking. They call it impossible, say nothing can change. And cynicism lives to infect another day. Or they think they can force other people to change. Or they carry on stoically trying to get people to change with methods that rarely succeed.

Making a difference differently

We need to find a different way of working with our differences – those we have with ourselves, our children, our work colleagues, customers, suppliers, next door neighbours, as well as those unfathomable people we see running across our TV screens in distant countries.

For many people, making a difference is bringing as many people as possible towards one way of thinking – a political solution, a community agreement, a united brand. It's called consensus. When reached, consensus is therefore the 'majority' view, often leaving the 'minority' view aside. Heard but ignored is as bad as being ignored altogether. Consensus is no sooner reached than the reasons for its existence have changed. People are seen to 'go back' on their agreement, 'breach' the contract. Trust is exploded and the forum for understanding why people have changed may be fatally compromised or not even be there at all. And unknown 'change' is seen to be the cause.

This perpetuates the vicious cycle of people looking upon change with suspicion and cynicism. Most people 'give up'. Others turn to aggressive or other forms of behaviour that deliberately go against the consensus. In the middle are society's decision-makers and those who recognise change and try to work with it – people who do know what they want to be different. Owing to the positions of passive apathy and active aggression around them, they struggle to actually make it happen. They see that they have fought their fight many times and the challenge is still there.

And this position – at which people choose to give up the 'fight', 'fight' within accepted boundaries, or 'fight' in ways that are unacceptable (simple undermining, cynicism, vandalising their workplace, throwing a sicky) – is exactly where Partnering can make a real difference.

The meaning of Partnering

'Partnering is an ethos that urges people and organisations to co-operate for mutual benefit – by challenging assumptions, raising affirmatively disruptive questions and embracing conflict.'

People have been asking me for a definition of Partnering and here it is. Over the last 12 years I have had the privilege of working with close to 30,000 people and I know that anything is possible – when people who think the situation is hopeless are challenged to stop giving up and recognise that things can be different.

I'm putting out this definition because I see the momentum for Partnering building. It's good news and it gives everyone in workplace and community organisations grounds for optimism.

Any definition can be challenged. A definition is simply an assumption of a shared meaning. A dictionary definition is only an assumption accepted by many people. Whatever, I am challenging people to see that they can take action to make things different.

Partnering is a liberating leap ahead

I believe that our futures rest in our ability to prompt change in ourselves through learning from others' differences. Here's where the leap of imagination occurs: if I know and believe that the core of what it means to develop is through noticing, understanding and learning from other people's differences, the way I then see the world can become an all-embracing vision. The implication is that we now need to find the skills that will enable people to prompt effective change in each other.

Adopting a Partnering ethos is an important quantum leap for our future, a necessary one for society's decision-makers who are only just beginning to understand what it might take to make diversity a reality and build inclusiveness into the business plan. Many have been grappling with developing effective internal change management strategies through empowerment and consultation, yet are still no nearer moving people through change effectively and sustainably.

In this book I'll be setting out tools, techniques and real-life examples of how to make Partnering part of your daily routine – in your organisation, your workplace, your life. I'll be discussing how adopting a Partnering ethos urges people and organisations to achieve amazing things. Starting with exploiting our capacity to be curious about what we notice, I'll explore the assumptions Partnering makes about what is possible. I'll be looking into the power of difference, the assumptions behind it and how we can embrace conflict for our own personal and organisational development. I'll introduce the conversational technique known as Affirmatively Disruptive Questioning and last but not least, I'll be encouraging you to get on and do it.

Change at the speed of success

For two decades, I've been a strategic business leader, focusing on organisational development and change, leadership and strategic partnerships, conflict management and team dynamics. I'm convinced that when people are trying to find a different path, most focus on the things that don't work very well. In my experience, we learn better from our successes, so I see my role as stopping people in their tracks and pointing them towards their possibilities – a social enabler, someone who helps people get curious enough to follow their passions.

All of my work is based on encouraging people in all kinds of organisations and communities to see the future in terms of possibility rather than fear. As individuals, we sometimes struggle to sustain our hopefulness. As individuals in communities we can gain some collective strength, working together to keep the possibilities alive – not by focusing on failure, but by remembering and repeating what works.

When people begin working with their passions it's completely liberating for them to suddenly realise they don't have to settle for mediocrity for themselves or anyone else, that they don't need world disasters or emergency situations to begin acting differently. I like giving people this powerful shock to their imagination. I have a vision for disrupting the way we see individuals, countries and continents so that we create for ourselves a different future.

Future = fear?

Isn't it amazing that we behave in this bizarre way, as if we believed this? In our organisations, we think about how to bring about the changes we need and immediately strive to prove that it is not a separate 'initiative'. People have learnt the power of calling something an initiative – it means I do not have to be engaged, it means it will not work, it means someone is out to catch me. Initiatives are not a bad thing. The world is changing fast, so it's for the best that organisations have the sense to change with it. If people say a change is not worth making because it will be a five-minute wonder, well, maybe that's exactly what it needs to be.

Many of society's decision-makers seem to believe that change is always hard, that it takes a long time, that people won't change. Maybe their biggest challenge is to think about who the change is directed at.

What on earth has created organisational cultures where endless time and resource is spent thinking about how to persuade people to see the value in changing, working differently, taking more responsibility, being innovative – and all the other things we keep desperately trying for? What is it about how most organisations operate that the people who wear cynicism as a badge of honour are given the most airtime?

People want change

Is there a need for people in organisations to see the world differently? Nobody wants the status quo   for the simple reason that none of us has ever lived in a time like today where the potential of what is possible is so high. We have more, we want more, we can achieve more. We will achieve more. As society, as organisations, as individuals, we drive onwards. We see that everything is possible. We drive further. We want change – for the better.

Driving onwards and upwards through so much change, we struggle to recognise and define success. Dare we imagine what our circumstances will be in a quarter of a century's time? We may not be able to imagine what life will be like in 25 days' time. Learning to live with that, to deal with it, to behave in the knowledge that there is little knowledge of the future, that everything will change, is a great new beginning.

For it to be successful, we need the leadership skills to support the positive exploitation of difference. And, since we are increasingly dependent on others to achieve success, that's quite a risk. So, how we think about risk in relation to the differences between people becomes central to our way of thinking.

There's an art to achieving this kind of success and it's called Partnering. Are you ready to cash in on conflict and succeed through Partnering?

How will you and your organisation do it? Simply put, most organisations that are still grappling with how to achieve effective internal change now need to find the skills that will enable them to prompt change in others. Partnering can and will liberate the way people work together for years to come.

CAN OF WORDS - LIBERATION

'Liberation' - it's a powerful word. It means different things in different contexts, so I don't use it lightly. When we apply the word to the organisations in which we work, does it imply that we are somehow imprisoned or trapped? If so, how, by what or whom? Stop for a moment and take 10 seconds to think about a situation, which you believe could be other than it is. It wasn't that difficult to find, was it? Sometimes we lose sight of what we are passionate about and cease to recognise the impact that we can have on others. When people begin working with their passions again it's completely 'liberating' for them to suddenly realise they don't have to settle for mediocrity for themselves or anyone else, that they don't need world disasters or emergency situations to begin acting differently. All it takes to make things happen is a shock to our imagination. Our imagination needs disrupting.

You'll never be the same again

Achieving success through Partnering means adopting a Partnering ethos. Adopting a Partnering ethos requires that we see the 'fight' we are engaged in differently. It challenges our notions of conflict. We all know what we mean by conflict. Or do we? To me, it's a representation of the differences between people. More than that. Conflict can be one of our greatest natural resources.

When we work together with a Partnering ethos we often come to realise that moving to a position of 'sameness' may not be the best possible outcome we could aim for. By hearing other people's differences and having our own differences heard, we may come to realise that we need a much better, more robust outcome than a fragile 'sameness' that takes the majority view as the one that must prevail at all costs.

Partnering poses one big question to anyone engaging with change in any way: how can we think about this differently so that we can make the difference we want to see?

The interesting thing about the Partnering ethos is that, once we catch a glimpse of what could be different, it compels us to persistently find opportunities to play with what could be possible.

Next time you travel and things are not working as you assume they should, take a sneaky peek at your fellow travellers. What assumptions do you make about their days, their lives and their journeys? Watch the aircrew – what assumptions do you hold about their motivation and reaction to the situation? How certain are you about the stories and fantasies you create? Perhaps you could commit the cardinal sin and start a conversation with your fellow traveller or long suffering aircrew!

Were your theories correct? What did you learn? You may still arrive late but, if you are anything like me, the person who meets you will be pleasantly surprised by the attitude you are adopting! There is no turning back. People who acquire the Partnering attitude will never be the same again.

2
Acquiring Attitude

Partnering urges
people and organisations
to achieve amazing things

There is no model for Partnering

The benefits and impact of acquiring a Partnering attitude mean that you can and will achieve what you want – the changes you want to see – and at lightning speed. Where do you start? With attitude and spirit. With ethos.

Acquiring the Partnering attitude is not like following a business model. Rather than a model, Partnering is an ethos that people need to commit to adopting and adapting – because every context is unique and any aspect of organisational or community life can benefit from it. Partnering recognises that working with the differences between people is what creates future possibilities for everyone. I have to be married to be a good husband. I need to work with my partner to know how to partner specifically with her. Without the 'other' I cannot determine what good Partnering is. Therefore, how can there be a model?

Every form of Partnering within an organisation and between organisations is going to be different and the context will always be unique. This is what makes me see that opportunities for innovation become endless, strategies become inevitably flexible and the capacity to understand differences from every angle – and exploit them – becomes the most highly prized commodity.

There is no aspect of business or community life that cannot benefit from the Partnering ethos.

> Partnering is about:
> - facing up to the differences and conflicts we have
> - dealing with them to maximise the benefits we can get from those differences
> - having the capacity to hold our views lightly and argue them through
> - creating the opportunity to find a solution that did not occur to either of us
> - having productive relationships with people anywhere, any time

And Partnering is about so much more. Although people will make their own sense of what an effective Partnering relationship is in their particular context, it is not only useful but important to set off from a common recognition of what Partnering is – a good reference point, a place to return to, a standard.

Partnering is not the easy option when working with difference

There is nothing airy-fairy or fluffy about acquiring the Partnering attitude. Here, we should not make the mistake of assuming that welcoming difference means anything goes, letting everything hang out, in an 'anything can happen' kind of way. The Partnering ethos carries an attitude and spirit that actively encourages the expression of opinions and the decision-taking that every business and organisation needs. It's a new, dynamic, disciplined, practical and sustainable approach based on assumptions. Far from being slow death by committee decision-making, Partnering is the most powerful way of driving things forward quickly that I've seen over the last decade.

Engaging in Partnering is tough. Let's be up front about that. Partnering is all about taking things head on instead of waiting until things break down. There will be internal conflict and we will be challenging each other.

Partnering takes courage

Acquiring the Partnering attitude takes courage – in your unique context. When our team worked with one of the major UK high street banks, we were with a group talking about principles of leadership. One principle discussed was 'Courage'. Two different people came up to us afterwards to say that they had really worked with this principle since our conversation and it had had a hugely positive effect. The first one said: "I saw that I needed to show more courage in my team meetings, to step up and voice my opinion, challenge where necessary and take decisions when the situation demanded. My team respect me more for it and we are performing much better."

Then the other person said: "I am proud of the way that I have shown my courage since that meeting. I used to have to be the first person and the last person to speak at my team meetings, to take the lead in making every decision and to challenge the ideas or approaches of others. I thought that was my job. After all, I am the boss. I've now taken the courage to trust in my colleagues – they're the experts who get on and do the real work, they should know best what we need to do. Of course, that does not mean that I have absolved myself of my responsibility. What it does mean is that we now work in a way where we consider the different ideas that people bring. I think we are now a real team and are performing much better."

This showed us that, in different contexts, courage means different things. There can be no prescriptive model for what it means to be courageous, or how to lead. The important thing is that we challenge ourselves and our assumptions.

Neither I nor anybody else can give you the solution or model of how to 'do' Partnering. As far as I am concerned, if you're prepared to acquire the Partnering attitude, there is no guidebook or training manual. I can give you a prompt about the questions you ask, challenge the assumptions you hold, help you to focus on what you are noticing and naming and the way you embrace conflict. And ultimately what makes Partnering achieve mutual benefit is determined and achieved by you and your partners – yourselves. A good place to start is by asking someone with whom you think you partner what makes your relationship effective. Take a chance – they may surprise you.

We can choose to lead and to follow

When something is as inevitable as the arrival of the Partnering ethos, we still have a choice of how we're going to meet it and treat it. As individuals, as teams, as companies, as communities, as nations, are we going to lead or to follow?

Many people in different contexts, from politics to business, will develop a Partnering ethos because they want positive and peaceful outcomes in which the differences between people are managed to create more possibilities. Others will increase their capacity to partner because they will see that an organisational capacity to work in this way may well become their future unique selling point. Could this be why one of the biggest UK public procurement programmes valued at £9 billion has allotted one third of the assessment criteria to Partnering capability? Traditionally, the assessment criteria in such public sector programmes have been wholly focused on cost and delivery. To base one third of the criteria on how people are going to work together shows huge foresight as well as an appetite for effective change. This particular organisation is choosing to lead the way.

Partnering includes the entire organisation

Assume you're including the whole organisation, because the business ethos of Partnering now demands that *entire organisations* become able to work in this way – and that is what is exciting, challenging and profoundly complex.

Partnering challenges so many of our assumptions – that only some people need to develop these skills, that people of a certain grade are incapable of thinking strategically, that people don't want to be valued and make a difference. I struggle to understand the wisdom of some leaders who fail to use the resources they have in their organisations – it's fascinating how easy it is to write people off.

I have seen this happen so many times and in so many organisations that I am spoilt for choice in terms of an example. Perhaps the most dramatic example is one of an organisation I worked with in South Africa. I was based at the time in the UK and working for an engineering organisation in Sweden (yes – you remember the airport lounge) – this time the call came from their head office asking me to go to South Africa to work with one of their companies there. This particular company had reported that there was a significant lack of supervisory and leadership skills, as much of its training budget was being given to literacy skills for the factory workers. During the late 1980s and early 1990s, after a long struggle, South African businesses were finally being encouraged to draw on the full resources of the people within the country – regardless of their colour. This reflected the growing momentum for change that was to finally result in the peaceful transition to democracy in South Africa.

The next few days were really interesting. Talk about assumptions! Because I had flown in from Stockholm the company representatives assumed I was Swedish – talk about not recognising a fellow countryman's accent! During those days members of the management team spoke Afrikaans whenever they wanted to talk about their experiences of working with Swedish consultants – so I learned rather more about company policy and ethos than they might have intended. On the third day I was speaking to one of the Union representatives and realised that one of the men on the shop floor had been involved in organising mass protests during the height of Apartheid – which he had started to do at the age of nine. So I was interested in how this organisation could be so clear that there were no leadership skills within it. If this was just one of the people from a group of 1,000 then just how many resources were not being used that were in fact available to that organisation?

I worked with the management team to help them recognise that they were addressing the wrong challenge. Their assumption had been that they lacked leadership potential. And yet there were strong, experienced and influential leaders all around them. Their real challenge was how they thought about the resources – yes, the people – around them. Once the management had addressed this issue, leading the organisation forward and engaging the workforce followed naturally.

How many organisations would cope if they created an environment where everyone was encouraged to bring their different strengths and partner with those around them?

Partnering requires a set of skills

As one of society's decision-makers, you will inevitably want to get on with acquiring the attitude. The challenge is… how? The only way we can tell others about this, introduce it to them, get the benefits, is by discussing what it would mean for us to partner together. We have to develop the skills and capacity to have a conversation with a potential partner to discover what a beneficial outcome for them would be, what assumptions they hold, what areas of conflict or difference we will need to grapple with – in the context of the relationship we have with them.

Getting into different kinds of conversations

Working with a project manager who is responsible for a £325 million project, we were discussing what it would take to ensure that the project was delivered on time and to budget. This particular project had a few interesting twists and turns. The people involved had just completed a previous project together that had ended up in court and in public inquiries – you might say that there were a few challenging historical relationships. It was a great example of viewing differences between others as an opportunity for positive exploitation.

In addition to the history, the number of stakeholders involved, public profile of the project and sheer size, all combined into the anticipation of yet another failed project in the minds of those involved. The conversation we were having focused on how the core team of 20 people from three different organisations could partner more effectively. Talking to me, the project manager made one of the most useful statements anyone in his position could make: "Charlie, what I do not want is a bunch of meetings where the team take away even more actions and develop even more processes to work well together – I just need them to think differently and then I know that they will make it happen." And that is the essence of what Partnering does.

We can only develop Partnering by co-operating with others and coming to a different way of thinking. This is what is so exciting about Partnering – it almost forces us into a great dialogue or conversation that we otherwise would not have. And before we know where we are, our position has changed, along with our actions.

Partnering will challenge the way you think

Acquiring the attitude will challenge the way you think and, therefore, the way you and your organisation do things. I was working with an organisation that was growing at a phenomenal pace. Using the parent company model, they had started their office with two people and had grown to over 100 employees within two years with an annual turnover in the multi-millions. They had developed a really strong culture where everyone knew each other on first name terms, there were many opportunities for people to learn more and adapt their skills, and the business was doing exceptionally well. The challenge they faced was too many emails, too many meetings, decisions were not being made quickly enough and the notion of the words 'work–life balance' in the same sentence was an anathema. They had even begun to notice that people were working more and more in silos, seldom consulting each other on changes that impacted on everyone.

They were facing many of the same dilemmas that large organisations find themselves in. The challenge for them was that business was doing well – and it was nearly killing them. In an attempt to be inclusive, e-mails were copied to almost everyone in the organisation and meeting invitations were sent out to anyone who could possibly have an interest. Leaving the office in the evening became more of a struggle as people constantly fought to get their 'day job' done.

Being asked to work with them on the issue of work–life balance seemed like the most obvious choice. However, this is not where the real issue lay. By paying attention to not only how their time was spent but also what was behind the things they were doing, they came very quickly to see that the solution lay not in the processes they had, but in the way they were thinking. Given the strong personal relationships between people, they were reluctant to disagree, raise issues or take a different point of view. This resulted in the endless e-mails, ineffective meetings and slowness of decision-making. As soon as people learnt to disagree, give their view and talk about their assumptions – including those about what was motivating individuals to behave in certain ways – there was a significant shift in the way people were working and the time it took.

One astounding example had to do with how they prepared for meetings with senior management. Individuals would literally spend hours preparing presentations to communicate their plans. I have seldom seen over 60 slides contain so much information, animation, graphics, statistics and font control. And each time someone slightly higher up the hierarchy would change something the domino effect led to yet more nights of customised animations. This was clearly an issue. A meeting was called – a new approach was needed – and so they discussed and sometimes argued for three hours about how to make presentations shorter, better ways to produce the facts, limiting the number of words on a slide… until finally, someone asked: "What is the purpose of these presentations?". The answers came thick and fast. Most brought them to the same conclusion, or was it an assumption? That's the way the boss wants it.

Here was their dilemma – were they prepared to challenge this way of doing things, that was taking literally hundreds of people hours for what they assumed was of benefit to one individual, even though that person was the head of the organisation? This is what Partnering requires. Noticing what we are doing and being prepared to challenge the assumptions that drive us – in a way that things can change.

The outcome for this organisation – as I see so often when things like this are challenged – was that the leader had no idea of the impact of a simple request he had made a year before, or what an industry it had become for people passionately trying to do a good job. People had failed to think about the purpose he was trying to achieve. This way of working had been introduced to push people to think logically and clearly, to encourage people to be succinct and precise, to bring a professional way of working into what had been a chaotic and unfocused way of making decisions. Of course, when everyone realised that what started as a good idea had turned into an industry, a different way of doing things was agreed. Is that the way it is in your organisation?

I wonder how many people are spending hours doing things that they believe you have asked for, really require or will hit the roof if you do not get whatever it is? Speak to any leader who has asked about something in passing only to discover that a project team is set up to put the answer together and you will know how often this happens. What are the assumptions your employees are currently working with? Some might shock you if you are prepared to ask!

Partnering is the business case for valuing difference

The big reason why acquiring the Partnering attitude provides such a strong business case is that its approach is essentially a systemic one that deals with complex differences and conflict head-on. Partnering works on so many levels: between customers and suppliers; between departments; within teams. It enables solutions to develop with the benefit of the collective intelligence of different people, departments, partners and business sectors.

How many times have you sat in negotiations and seen that there is simply no possible option for a Win-Win solution?

Win-Win moves to Both-Gain

Partnering drives us beyond Win-Win to Both-Gain outcomes. We arrive at a Both-Gain outcome when we avoid determining what winning is before we even talk to our partners – or the 'other side', as we sometimes call them. If one of the most profound ways to learn and develop is through others' differences, then what on earth makes us think that we are getting the best we possibly can by formulating our idea of a win before tapping into the diverse expertise of the other side?!

Win-Win is a bit like both parties getting what they originally wanted without realising they could get a whole lot more. I might decide that something I need or want is so outside of what is possible, I don't even go there – only to discover months later that it was the easiest thing in the world for me to sort out. To drive for Both-Gain also means putting a great big elephant foot on the notion of hidden agendas. We all have agendas. Let's just get them out there, use the differences and get to Both-Gain.

CAN OF WORDS – WIN-WIN

How many times in your life has the tempting scenario of Win-Win been dangled before you? What seems like a fantasy, or at the very least an oxymoron, rarely comes to fruition in real life. If we bothered to analyse our involvement in such an improbability, we might begin to realise that it is only the 'I win' half of the bargain that we're at all interested in. If we could get past what we consider winning to be, however, perhaps we could begin to appreciate the reality rather than the fantasy. After all, Win-Win is a concept in which curiosity about the other half of the bargain hardly exists.

In our working lives, we have become used to different models of behaviour, of which the most positive is this Win-Win scenario. Partnering is a philosophy that liberates us from the models we have imposed on ourselves, our communities and organisations. It helps us see the world differently: change is possible, we can learn from difference and work well with conflict.

Working with a printing company that was facing ever-increasing prices for paper and a paper merchant unable or unwilling to reduce the cost of the paper, I saw first hand the meaning of Both-Gain. In a coffee break people were chatting and stumbled across a staggeringly simple yet rewarding alternative. The paper merchant would deliver paper through the night around the country. Once the paper was delivered his trucks would return to the depot. The printer was spending large sums of money on distribution of printed goods. By setting up a system of 'back-loading', which meant loading up the trucks that were newly empty having just delivered the paper with printed goods, the printer reduced his operating costs. More than that, he kept his paper price and his customers, and those two organisations had laid a strong foundation for their future.

For Partnering to be successful, we need to try to see our world as one whole system. Our focus needs to be on the relationships between organisations nurtured by individuals, rather than relationships between a few key individuals despite their organisations' systems. We need strategic thinking and systems that support the Partnering way of working and liberate EVERYONE in the organisation to see the world differently and act accordingly.

It is certainly what I absolutely yearn for every time I am faced with the video shop and its systems. I can begin to understand people driven to acts of extreme behaviour as I see a distraught mother with three arguing kids struggling to find a DVD that will bring peace in the house for a few hours and the conversation with the video staff going something like: "Look, Mrs Robinson, I know you've been coming here for years, that I recognise you and that my daughter is supposed to be coming to your house to watch this DVD, but our system means that if you do not have your card or passport with you I cannot hire out the DVD to you." And these are the same organisations that tell me their staff just work there for the money, do not have the skills to lead and so on.

Curiosity kills the catatonia

Acquiring the attitude takes curiosity about the assumptions we all make when trying to make a difference. After all, the differences between us lead us to an interplay of assumptions. You made one when you saw the title of this book. In turn, I anticipated your assumption and made several more of my own when structuring this book. Maybe what both of us noticed was different to what we now notice. How would we know unless we asked each other directly? Now, that could be interesting.

I'm very curious about the assumptions we all make when we're trying to make a difference. I look at the pressures on society's decision-makers – how you're constantly expected to find different ways to engage, motivate, make things meaningful for people. Aren't leaders supposed to be people who enable others to do great work? Isn't a good leader one who creates a culture where everyone else can take the lead? There is a blame culture in our organisation/community/world and, of course, who created it but our senior leaders and society's decision-makers?

You're a leader – isn't it your job to take me out of my catatonic trance of boredom and make my life interesting?

For some time now, such assumptions have seemed less and less useful. If we are questioning the assumptions we hold, are there any assumptions that are useful for Partnering, given that there is no model for it?

As nobody benefits from a Partnering relationship alone, perhaps one of the first and most powerful assumptions is that, when we do find a new way to gain from our interactions with others, it is a profound route to our development and the development of others. And what better way to do that than by adopting a curious attitude?

3
Noticing
Chaos

Partnering makes us curious, not angry, about what we notice

Notice how you notice

I was working on a programme sponsored by the Cabinet Office in the UK called Leaders in Partnership. The aim of the programme was to work with senior civil servants to assist them in managing the range of complex partnerships that is the reality of working in the public sector in the UK. On this particular programme we adopted a somewhat different approach. We invited a group of sixth form pupils (about 15 or 16 years old) from a local school and this group worked with the adults for the week as a way of developing cross-generational relationships for the development of both groups.

A key element of the programme involved the group going to visit a local community and spending the day talking with people and noticing how things worked. At the end of the day the group gave feedback to that community, helping them to see what was working and what could be different. The group learned to develop the crucial skill of noticing and the art of describing things in a way that helps people to act differently.

At the beginning of the time together I asked the group to go out of the room and work on their own for 15 minutes and then come back – the simple task was to go out and notice what you notice. Hearing what people reported on their return showed that this was truly fascinating for the group. Of course there were differences between everyone's feedback – and there was also a clear distinction between what the young people and the adults tended to see. One of the reflections that most startled and disturbed the group was that the young people used language of hope and possibility and were significantly more positive in what they saw.

They spoke of seeing the clouds as the promise of snow, the free coffee and snack vending machine, the fun the gardeners were having making a bonfire and the warmth they got from standing near it – they saw life and energy around them. This contrasted sharply with the comments of the senior leaders, society's decision-makers, who seemed much more inclined to notice the deficit. They told of a building needing repair, of the health and safety hazard of the bonfire so close to the trees, the grey skies and miserable people wandering around the property.

And when the group noticed the differences between what they were saying, how did they react? Were they fascinated about the different perceptions that people held?

Not really. The group started arguing about the facts – who was right and who was wrong – just stopping themselves short of rushing out the room again to 'prove' what they had noticed.

In a Partnering context we need to be noticing what we are noticing, and not excluding the possibility that others might be noticing something different – possibly even something that seems contradictory. And both of us can be right.

There are myriad meanings to an event and even more ways to describe it. In any situation we will see (or not see) many things around us. And we will describe those things either in our heads or to others. We all have experience of being with someone and they tell us about something they saw. We were also there and either had not noticed or had noticed but would describe it in a very different way.

As a matter of fact

We are accustomed to people describing situations as if everything were hard fact. In fact, many people start their stories with the two words that started this sentence. Some of us hear alarm bells whenever the word 'fact' is mentioned – especially if we're concerned to get at a deeper meaning. 'In fact, my manager did something he wasn't supposed to do.' 'In fact, he dislikes me intensely.' 'In fact, I'm going to resign.' 'In fact, fancy a coffee?'

I am reminded of a family mediation situation that I found myself in. It sticks in my memory in particular because it was a daytime television show. You know, one of those 'My teenage daughter is an aubergine' shock-horror-confrontation-for-all the-family shows.

Anyway, the family concerned consisted of a mother, two boys and a girl. The dispute centred around an event the previous week where one of the boys had hit the mother with a plank.

How come so much of the shouting, arguments and discussion concerned the thickness of the plank, instead of what had created a situation where someone would hit someone else with a plank – and their mother, at that?

So, what you notice is not always what I notice. And often my instinct is to feel that in order for me to be confident in my reality of the world, I need to contest yours – as though it were an 'either/or' situation. Because, let's face it, arguing over the facts can seem a great deal easier than having to deal with a world that might be a different place for different people. Of course, when we explain and describe what we notice, everything will become so much clearer, wont it?

Lost in translation

The common factor is that, most of the time, we all seem to want other people to understand that we mean what we say. So, how come this is so often misunderstood? Lost in translation? By people who can speak the same language? Actually (there's one of those 'factual' words, again), that's exactly what it is – lost in translation. In the act of communicating something we hold to be true, certain aspects tend to lose the sense we intended to give them. There is a big gap between fact and meaning.

Are people listening for facts or are they listening for meaning? Isn't listening a form of interpretation?

How we interpret something depends on the context. While it's clear that people derive meaning from the facts, everything depends on the context. The sudden thought 'Footsteps behind me' produces different reactions in people who put themselves in that position. 'Footsteps behind me when shopping' and 'Footsteps behind me at 2am' can produce entirely different reactions in different people. You might be quite unconcerned to hear footsteps behind you at two in the morning, whereas I might be quite scared. These feelings might reverse in different circumstances.

On one level I know that you will find the above example obvious – and I use it intentionally. What about some of the less obvious examples? The next time you are in a meeting that's going round in circles, or preparing to give someone difficult feedback, or on your way home convinced that the position you took in this morning's argument at home remains justified – remember the footsteps at 2am. What should or could you be noticing about the meaning you and others are giving? How helpful is it to assume a different position?

Far from 'fact', what we notice is voluntary – we can choose to notice different things and then choose again how we name what we have noticed. All of this is driven by the assumptions we hold – which in turn are optional. If we hold this as a reality in even half of our interactions then it can both liberate and scare us. If I assume that what I notice and how I describe it are not voluntary, then I am free of taking responsibility for my actions and what I do. If I take responsibility for what I see, then my role in the world takes a different shape. Perhaps this can mean that sometimes you surprise yourself – and possibly others.

Notice the impact of what you notice

One of the most effective ways to assume the Partnering position is to start paying attention to the notion of noticing. What is it that prompts different people to notice different things? Prompts others to not notice at all? Prompts yet more of us to have 'notice over-load'?

How much can you understand people and yourself by listening to the way we describe what we notice and the language we use to describe it?

The challenge to every individual and organisation adopting a Partnering ethos is that you need to be prepared to start noticing what you notice, being conscious of how you describe or name what you see and to become fascinated by how others notice and name what you both see. When Partnering, one of the most valuable skills is the ability to get infinitely curious about the chaos of human noticing and engaged by the art of spotting the possible.

You might reasonably say: 'So what? You notice what you notice and I will stick to my own reality. What difference does it make?'

When our senior civil servants from the story above reflected on this question they considered how what they noticed influenced their actions. Now, this was a bunch of very important people. They controlled budgets. They set policy. They are society's decision-makers, and, of course, the decisions they make are influenced by what they notice. So our world is shaped. If we notice only vandalism, we smother our cities with barbed wire. If we notice only inefficiencies we get an increased number of controls. If we notice only hopelessness – then perhaps the best thing to do is to write off that community and invest our limited resources elsewhere where we do believe we can make a difference.

When we challenged the senior leaders to notice some of the things that their youthful partners were noticing – the hope and the energy and the life – then new possibilities started to emerge.

Before you sink back into the comfort of your cynicism at childish spin doctoring, knowing that when they grow up they will learn, let yourself for one moment think about what you tend to notice, how you describe it and the impact you are having on those around you. This is not about simply changing the language you use to describe what you have always seen. It is not about the smirk that people get on their faces as they describe a hideous task to someone as a development opportunity. If my starting point is that partners cannot be trusted then no amount of meetings and workshops, where we agree that trust is important to our work together, is going to have any impact.

Don't always take me literally!

While we are on the subject of cynicism, if there is one phenomenon that makes absolutely no sense to me it is the situation where entire organisations hostage themselves to the opinions of a few cynics – some would say that entire nations do something similar in the way their media works. I have seen entire organisational change programmes designed around these few individuals. Given such power it is little wonder that these people hold onto their point of view so tightly, claiming that things will never change. But they can – if we believe it and have the courage to challenge.

I was working on a Leading to Excellence programme for 90 leaders in an organisation. The group was discussing the impact that cynics have in the organisation. Later that month I joined the Board for its Leadership Development day. As we sat down to lunch the CEO said: "Oh Charles, you will be pleased to know that our people are doing what you told them to and it has worked really well." Before my head and chest had time to begin their swelling process, he added:

"What made you think of getting them to put up signs around Bill's desk saying 'DON'T INFECT ME WITH YOUR CYNICISM'?"

Well, coleslaw has never travelled down my throat so quickly. I know that I have some whacky strategies, but that one seemed a bit extreme even for me! I finally worked out that I had said something about getting really angry when organisations and people let a few cynical people infect them. The group had heard that as an invitation from me to communicate this with Bill, who, by the way, I had neither met nor heard of. Thankfully, he saw the funny side and has apparently changed his behaviour.

I remain firm, however, that this is an approach I am not suggesting! We can choose which voices we hear and give authority to in our organisations. Sometimes it seems to me that we only give credibility to the 'old lags' – the lifers who say: 'We tried that before. It did not work then and it won't work now. Give up. Things will never change. They never listened to us. We are all doomed.' You can probably picture the people I am talking about. And what about innovation, optimism and possibility – how do we nurture them, to give them life, too?

Name what you notice... with care

Isn't it better to use life-giving language, rather than the language of deficit? Using a turn of phrase that our favourite wordsmith loves, when we start paying attention to what we notice and how we describe it, we begin to open a whole can of words. When we name things we can tend to do this in a way which limits people, rather than enabling them to do great work. In a manner that accuses rather than explores their passions. We even use words that maintain the current state we are desperate to change.

I was working with the leader of an internal consultancy organisation. With over 1,000 people in his part of the organisation, supporting and consulting to an organisation of 180,000 people, he was grappling with how to change the overall organisational culture.

He was animated as he described what needed to change. People were not taking the initiative, they were not entrepreneurial enough, there were too many layers in the organisation. As I often do, I began asking him about the things that made him proud of working in this organisation – and he was off. "Well, you know, Charlie, every morning we mobilise over 100,000 people throughout the country, our troops are out there. When I was in the operation my command was one of the largest." And so he went on. I began to reflect on the impact of calling teams 'commands', naming people as troops, going to war!

Now, it's been well known for decades that military metaphors have overtaken the English language to such a degree that even the most peace-loving conscientious objectors use them in everyday situations. Yet, it's a second nature that has consequences for how we think and act at high levels. In meetings, someone is determined to 'lead from the front' before they 'close ranks'. If it doesn't work, we say 'Next time, we'll need to bring the heavy artillery.' With a smile we add: 'Bill's the one to apply the thumbscrews.' Torture?! We all do it. And here I was noticing it in someone in a position of changing organisational culture! The funny thing is, the form of communication known as language tends to make everything more, not less complicated. The language we then use to describe what we notice (even when we are using the same dialect or language) seldom holds the same meaning or significance for others.

Yet we tend to take for granted that we have a common understanding of what is being said and rarely take the time to check it out. Every word or phrase can carry a nuance or a meaning that packs a surprise. How come, for example, in the English language, the term 'do-gooder' has come to mean the very opposite in so many people's minds?

What use is language if words mean their exact opposite?

After all, if you're not a 'do-gooder' are you a 'do-badder'? Or perhaps you're a 'do-nothing-at-aller'? If you were teaching someone, a non-English speaker, our language, where would you start to translate this phrase?

CAN OF WORDS – ENGLISH

I admire people who can speak foreign languages, because much of my time is spent translating English into English. I've noticed among British and American people (or anyone using the universal business language that English has become) that, when it comes to understanding each other, there is an inherent assumption that, because we speak the same language, there is only ever one definition for every word. People have become very reluctant in any conversation to ask the meaning of a word. This kicks off a huge game of assumptive language, because people make all kind of assumptions around what others mean. People need to have the courage to check the meaning that others are giving to certain words. People have emotional connections to words. Words are wonderful things. They might have a dictionary definition, but in a specific context, spoken by someone in particular, that word will hold a particular meaning. Rather than consult the dictionary, there is only one real way to find out. Ask. We all have to be our own interpreters and translators and get better at both roles.

How to get curious, not angry

Recognise the chaos of communication

These stories of noticing, of different realities and the power of language, remind me again that no matter how clear you think you are, there will be multiple ways that people hear and understand what you say. The challenge is how we get really curious about these times rather than angry. As soon as I say that, I can immediately think of countless situations where I have done anything but get curious about what someone does or says. On the odd occasion that I do start to think differently, I have found the notion of trying to understand what is driving my behaviour and that of others quite useful.

When you think about how communication between two people works, what is the picture that comes to your mind? Take a moment and think about this. If you have a pen and paper handy, draw a diagram. How do you represent communication? What does it look like?

Often people's response to this task is based around straight lines. Lines between 'stick people', lines between smiling or frowning faces. Sometimes the lines are messy and confusing and zigzag all over the place. Perhaps there are pictures of big mouths and tiny ears. Maybe your image is more symbolic, or involves feelings and emotions.

This is how communication looks to me. I see each person standing in their own world and the world they are creating together. Each person brings all of their past highlighted by the present and tickled by the future. I can almost see a starburst behind each person's head – there are fireworks, explosions, all sorts of connections being made. In the midst of that chaos, the words between the two are exchanged, understood and misinterpreted. And finally, I walk out of the newsagent's with my morning paper, completely unaware that I have engaged with another human being at all, yet clear that I always go to that shop because the people there are so nice.

Overall, communication between people operates on a number of different levels at the same time. On one level we know from our experiences that communication is chaotic and yet it still seems to surprise us and we call it miscommunication. We seem to have a kind of 'send and receive' model in our brains. We use metaphors about 'posting' information, as though this involves a simple delivery of meaning from one person to another. Our mental model implies that communication is simply the coding and decoding of the message that is sent. The only problem with these linear type models is that there is an assumption that communication is straightforward, which, in my experience, it seldom is. This is often how communication is represented, as sending information from one person to another in a straightforward fashion. Most models of communication do not model what actually happens. What does this model imply?

What are our assumptions about this model? First, we assume that we think about what we say. I don't know about you but I cannot claim that this is always the case. Then this assumes that the message is sent in exactly the same way that we thought about it. When it gets to the other person, this model assumes they interpret the message correctly and neutrally. And finally, it implies that the message was received, understood and acted on in the way that it was originally thought about. There are lots of assumptions here and most of the time we see that this model doesn't work – we have created a model of communication that doesn't help us in reality.

If we accept that communication can be closer to chaos than anything the linear model intimates, it is valuable to consider the following:

- we no longer accept or assume that communication is straightforward
- we recognise the potential for confusion
- there is always something that has a significant influence on how we adopt the meaning we do
- if we pay attention to these significant influences, there are ways to increase the possibilities for successful communication

A great example of the chaos and how our lives influence our communication, involves our colleague Gillian. As a result of a demanding travel schedule with her work, Gillian is often away from home and her young family for weeks at a time. At the time of this incident, she had been away for two weeks. The evening prior to her return home she was attending a reception hosted by her organisation, and having a chat with me, my colleague Graeme and a Russian colleague, Tatiana. The conversation had turned to gardening and Gillian said she was looking forward to having a vegetable patch the coming spring. She mentioned that she already had strawberries growing in her lawn and that her two little boys loved to go into the garden and eat them. At this point, Tatiana remarked: "You better be careful, if you don't take care of them they will grow wild". Gillian looked sharply at Tatiana and said slowly: "Oh, really?" The conversation took a particularly icy turn. Witnessing the exchange, Graeme and I burst into laughter. Of course, Tatiana, a gardener herself, was talking about the strawberries, concerned that unless they were pruned and managed carefully, the plants would shoot and the fruit crop would suffer. Now Gillian had heard something completely different – and was shocked that her trusted friend and colleague should be questioning her parenting abilities in this way!

So, while it is useful to start with a notion of chaos around communication, the things that are influencing our lives, big and small – our priorities, our concerns, our desire to make it home in time to get our daily dose of our favourite soap opera – are all things that influence how we communicate.

When the 'chaos' occurs, how do we increase our capacity to resist the irritation and the frustration that we have been misunderstood and take the time to consider what it might be that is going on – for us or for the others involved?

How do we use appreciation, good will and good intent to understand the chaos of communication?

Understand what makes us TIC

I have come to see that what people notice and how they describe what they notice is greatly affected by the significant influences on their life at that particular moment in time. Of course, at one level, this is common sense, simple common sense. And the other thing I know is that common sense often abandons me when I most need it.

One of the handy prompts I have come to rely on over the years is one that helps me to claw back my common sense in those infuriating moments when people accuse me of letting my children grow wild and communication has flown out of the window. I call it the TICing model. As a tool that helps us to stop and think in the chaos of communication and to get curious not angry, it has proved to be a valuable tool for people entering a world of Partnering. And the great thing is that it seems to be useful and applicable to people irrespective of their culture or home language.

Now before I start to describe it, a word of reassurance. It is simply a tool, to be used only when you need it. Think about when you're considering using a map. When I am clear on where I am going then I do not consult a map. It is when I get lost that I want to briefly check that my sense of where to go is right or whether I have completely lost my way and I really need to use this map.

At its most basic, the TICing model is a map that provides you with a range of prompts to think about what might be influencing you in any given context – help you to make sense of yourself, if you like – and encourages you to become curious about the world around you. The fun thing is that every single person carries with them their own model, TICing away, influencing their thoughts and deeds – whether they know it is there or not. So, with TICing models there is a significant health warning. When you get familiar with it, you can become quite good at understanding your own TICing model. And much as I would dearly love to understand exactly what makes someone else TIC at any one time (like situations of air rage), I cannot possibly know without asking. So, the TICing model is for us a means of creating a hypothesis about what might be influencing others – a guess that can then guide us in the questions we may ask them.

Let me draw on a story that a friend of mine tells of his curious conversation with his wife one Saturday night. I wonder how many of you will be able to see some element of your own interactions in this example of what makes people TIC. Doris and Paul are going out to a party. Doris is (finally) ready. Comes down the stairs. Paul is standing at the front door, ready to leave and says: "You look good. Is that top new?" Doris turns on her heel, muttering: "If I look fat, I need to get changed." She goes back upstairs. Paul is left standing there, thinking, 'What happened? What did I say? Has the world gone mad?' It seems to him a completely illogical conversation. He has the wisdom not to pursue it there and then.

A couple of weeks later, he thinks about it and recalls something that happened on their recent holiday in China. He pictures the great modern markets in China that sell the sort of clothes that Doris loves to wear. They'd spent a long time going around the boutiques and stalls. Wherever they went Doris would ask: "Have you got this in my size?" And, being shopkeepers, they would of course say yes.

Now, Doris is not a big woman, she's tall and slim. But in China, the clothing is made for the local market, which is typically smaller than Doris. She tried dress after dress, top after top and all were – just – too small. She would look hopefully at Paul and ask: "Is this OK?" and Paul would respond: "Can you breathe?" Doris would hand back the clothes to the shopkeeper. Paul thought the shopping in China was great – very economical.

After a few frustrating trips, Doris gave up, saying she was not going to humiliate herself anymore, fighting with clothes in tiny enclosed boutiques, with immaculate-looking petite women making her feel like a huge bloated freak. And that was the end of it. Until that curious Saturday night.

When Paul remembers all this, he realises that, probably subconsciously, when he'd said: "Is that top new?" Doris's recent association with new clothes was of being the oversized and unattractive one, bursting out of something too small. In that situation, it was only logical that she should take offence and go to change. Paul learnt all about Doris's TICing model on that day the hard way.

And that's the point – that is what makes communication so wonderfully fascinating and frustrating at the same time. It is in that moment that we may come to understand what makes us and others TIC and then the next day it can be completely different. When we are Partnering with others we need to see that people's reactions and behaviour will shift and change. Seeing that we need to understand what drives this – rather than instantly losing trust in them – is what it is about.

Broadly speaking, you can consider the range of significant influences as three categories. Time. Internal. Context. These are what make us TIC – hence our TICing model. Remember, the model is simply a map, a prompt to help us recognise and pay attention to the different obstacles and pathways for great conversation.

The TICing model

Time. When things happen might have a significant influence on how we think, feel or interact in any particular moment. What is making you TIC right now? Maybe there is an influence of time. Could it be that your child came top of the class yesterday and you are still glowing with pride so much that you want to phone all your friends, rather than read a book? Perhaps your glasses are at the optician's today, so you are finding it difficult to concentrate, reading using an old pair? Maybe you have a meeting that you think might be problematic tomorrow, so you are deeply engrossed in this chapter because you think that this model might help you to make it a success.

Internal. Each of us brings our own unique take on the world, our own priorities, views and expectations. Perhaps it is one of these internal triggers that is making you TIC most loudly at the minute. Is there an assumption that is making a noise – did you assume TIC should be spelt TICK and now you can't find the K? Is there something to do with your role? If you are reading this book with an expectation that you will have to teach the contents to your colleagues, the pressure of that role might have a significantly different influence than if you are simply in the role of reader. What about your values, those deeply held beliefs? Perhaps you prioritise honesty and, as you read, you are excited as you see that this tool enables a greater degree of self-honesty.

Context. The situation that we are in, literally, metaphorically or culturally can have the primary influence on how we are. Are you reading this on the bus? If so, you might be distracted by the need to look up and check your whereabouts every time the bus comes to a halt – you don't want to miss your stop. Perhaps you are in a library – ordinarily, maybe you like to annotate the books you read, highlight the highlights and draw faces – but those librarians tend to frown when you do that with library books. Maybe the culture at work is one where action is valued above all else and the simple act of reading a book prompts you to feel guilty – however relevant it might be to your job.

Of course, some people would see the old reading glasses as being a context. Or not defacing library books as a value of respecting other people's property. Doesn't matter. It is only a map to help us to recognise what might be there, TICing away, influencing us at any time. Or getting curious about someone else. And if you don't need to know in this situation, don't even take the map out of the glove box. And remember, if you did notice something that is making you TIC, right now, don't take it for granted. Tomorrow, the chances are it will be something else. Maybe it has changed already.

Notice what's TICing you off

To acquire a Partnering attitude you will need to pay a great deal of attention to TICing models. It's a form of self-noTICing. How can others ever know what we think when we are often not that clear ourselves? No wonder we live in a world of communication chaos!

My friend Mark (otherwise known as our wordsmith) says he has learned more about the effect of his words on others in the last year than in the previous 45 years of his life. And he describes himself as a wordsmith. He told me he was at the hairdresser's the other day, for once enjoying the lively atmosphere in the place. Usually, it's dead as a doornail and a vast effort to engage the hairdresser in any conversation more meaningful than the price of hair gel ('*why* do I keep going there?' he asked himself – '*because* I'm too lazy to look for someone else…' – not a particularly effective answer).

The reason for the liveliness was a child running up and down, laughing and playing, picking up bits of hair off the floor. "Nice and lively in here today," Mark said to the hairdresser. And the hairdresser replied: "Yes, sorry about that – it's the last time I'm going to allow someone to bring in their child, making all this fuss. I realise that people like you want a bit of peace when they come in." His 'answer' stopped Mark in his tracks. It made him question just how many other people heard his 'straightforward' statements as irony.

How we hear anything is inextricably linked to our personal experience. Perhaps one of the hairdresser's parents had regularly scolded him for making a noise as a child. Perhaps the hairdresser's general conversations were of the ironic kind in which people say the opposite of what they mean. Mark hadn't intended to make a 'neutral' or an ironic statement and was only trying to communicate something he liked. But, he could never know how the receiver would hear it, because he did not know everything that was making him TIC.

When people get to know us, they're all used to asking each other, "How's your TICing model today?"

It's a quicker, better and more relaxed way of getting a conversation off in a useful way.

The challenge to every individual and organisation adopting a Partnering ethos is that you need to be prepared to be brave to notice and name and respond to things differently.

If you don't at least try, you bring about 'no change' and you are responsible for things being the way they are – a legacy of the past, with you and your organisation backing into the future, or forward into the past, depending on your point of view.

Although Partnering is familiar as a term, many people do not yet have the skills to ensure that it creates possibilities and develops effective long-term relationships. So people need to learn how to work within this very complex business approach. Partnering skills can be learned very quickly. Once we pay attention to noticing and naming what we see, getting a handle on what on earth makes us TIC (and others, for that matter) the next skill area concerns being explicit about the assumptions we hold and exploring new assumptions we could hold about Partnering, while Partnering.

4

Adopting Assumptions

Partnering makes some powerful assumptions about what is possible

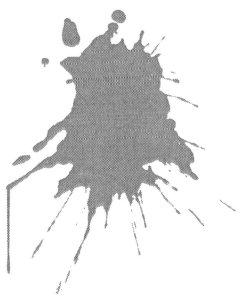

What is an assumption?

When working in a way that focuses on Partnering with others, we can see how many assumptions we all make – most of which we never even notice and are useful and some of which turn us upside down.

Are our assumptions mostly things we take for granted, that we take to be true based on our reality and experiences, guesses that sometimes need no effort?

What on earth?

A core element of the British Council-sponsored African InterAction leaders programme is a series of amazing events where over 100 representatives from 19 African countries and the UK gather together in one location for three days.

For the British Council staff and pan-African facilitation team these are 18-hour days during which time we experience a range of things from elation to frustration. At one of these events the decision was taken to hold another event in Accra, Ghana. Anyone who has lived, travelled or worked in Africa will know that it is far easier to fly from a European country to an African country than to travel within Africa. So, apart from the other normal challenges of organising an event of this nature, helping so many people to travel to Ghana was a real challenge. When the facilitation team arrived in Ghana and engaged in very vocal greetings, our British Council project manager had one of those looks on his face. One of the things I have come to learn on this project is that when he looks like that I cannot hope to assume what has happened and know that his response will start with OK, no problem.

It turned out that the reason our project manager was looking the way he did was that there had been a misunderstanding with the hotel about the dates. A day before we were due to start he was 50 bedrooms short for our participants for the last night and we had no plenary room for the last day. Normally, with the number of hotels in Accra, this would have been manageable. However, on the very week we were there it was also the Economic Community of West African States (ECOWAS) Justice Ministers Conference. The city was overrun with ministers and their many entourages and all hotels were telling us they were full. Picture the scene as our project manager worked hard to resolve the hotel issue while the participants started to arrive and register.

One of our participants from east Africa took great exception to the fact that his name was spelt wrongly on his badge and refused to wear it. He had a long and heated argument with the woman at the registration desk. For the next few days he raised this issue with all the male facilitators on the team and in the plenary room. His key issue was with ineffective and stupid administrators who were disrespecting his identity as a man, that women should not be allowed to do this and so on and so forth.

Our project manager pulled all the stops out to find enough rooms for our participants. We were very grateful for the effort he made. Our task, however, was then to find a way of helping the participants to see the great opportunity in moving for the last night to a hotel one hour away from the venue and three stars below the standard of the one we were in. Thankfully, we had just run the session on assumptions that placed particular emphasis on appreciation, good will and good intent. After an engaging and very long cultural night our participants were taken back to their hotel.

The next morning, as the facilitation team prepared for the day, much of our time and thoughts were taken up by working out how to deal with our participants on their return. We made a number of assumptions: they would be late, as our co-ordinator had apparently assumed we would start at a different time to all the other five events we had run; that the participants would not be happy with their accommodation, as we had heard there was no hot water, that. . .

As we walked to our new plenary room (which had been a Thai restaurant the night before), we heard much commotion and noise outside. It was 30 minutes before we were due to start, so we followed our curiosity and went outside. There were our participants coming out of their bus and a troupe of dancers performing for them, press taking photographs and everyone waving at members of the public looking on. Talk about assumptions! Their hotel manager had heard that they were leaders and assumed that they were the ministers for the ECOWAS conference. Not wanting them to be late, he had called the police and demanded an escort through the city. Whizzing through the city, our participants had had a fine time feeling like ministers. And, of course, when they arrived at the hotel, the press, dance troupe and public assumed they were the ministers as well!

With a much relieved facilitation team we prepared for a calmer day with one assumption left – that we still had to manage our east African man and his ego. In the plenary session on that final day he spoke about his reaction to the spelling of his name, how he had made assumptions about people not respecting him and recognised that through the conflict and the way people responded to him that he had a choice about what he focused on. And, with much grace, he ended by saying one had to be careful of the pressure we put on administration people. The team smiled and I pointed out as gently as possible that it was great he was thinking differently and might find it useful to know that the registration person was in fact a pilot on the Ghana airlines. She had given her time to help and was doing everything she could to ensure that all of our participants got home to their own countries. And, of course, what does this say about the assumptions we make about people and what they are capable of, let alone what their role says about what they are able to do?

We all do it

We all hold assumptions – they guide our thinking and actions all the time. They can have a significant influence on our TICing model – they are part of our *internal* constitution that guides us in life. As human beings, we have grown up having learned to hold myriad assumptions – most of which we never even have reason to bring into focus. Quite often, we don't even realise we are making assumptions. So we don't see that what we are doing is taking a risk.

One thing that never ceases to astound me is the number of assumptions that are made in the world of business. There are times when I sit in on meetings and, if I were to be throwing a ball of wool to each person as they made yet another statement, criticism, decision or conclusion based on unspoken and untested assumptions, we would not be able to see each other for knitting within the hour. One of the most damaging assumptions is that I will look stupid if I ask a question or check out an assumption I am making.

Every morning, we make a thousand assumptions before we get to work. My children have arrived at school safely. There will be coffee beans for the machine. A red light means the traffic will stop to let me cross the road. The train will arrive and take me where I need to go. The fair trade coffee I'm drinking will benefit disadvantaged farmers in Venezuela. The newspaper I'm reading will make me laugh rather than depress me. Once at work, with sufficient caffeine we up the pace on the positions we assume.

Where do we get our assumptions from?

We get our assumptions in so many ways and, in my view, mostly through good reason and good intention. People offer us a view of the world that they think will benefit us and so we learn our assumptions from experience.

Often because we inherit our assumptions from parents or authority figures and through our experience we come to see them as 'facts' – my father told me to study hard so that I could get a good job to secure my future; my grandfather said, "Be a self-made man, never rely on someone else for your income." This need not lead to fights or penury respectively, but it does highlight to us that these are assumptions we can accept or discard.

What we focus on becomes our reality. It's the result of one or more of our assumptions. As a child, I remember that my Irish grandmother would walk along the street and, as she passed a young man, would say: "That poor wee man!" And then she would be off: "He is struggling to find a job, his mother is probably ill and needs help, and as for that father of his, he has turned to drink."

Amazed that she knew this person so well, I would ask his name. Oh, she did not know him from Adam – these were just the assumptions she was making and reinforcing to herself in the way she expressed them. He was probably an astronaut on his day off, looking for some personal space.

At least I knew what my grandmother was thinking – she voiced her views. As we all have to make assumptions, what is important is that we make our assumptions explicit, in business as anywhere else.

In a meeting where there is stalemate, to help the conversation move on could we ask: "What assumptions are we holding?"

It could be the most useful question we ever ask.

CAN OF WORDS – EQUAL

Managers in many organisations feel they have been forced to take on the assumption that 'everyone is equal', when they know that this is far from their experience. They feel that employee legislation compels them to treat everyone the same. Partnering recognises that people are not the same. There is a difference between this and saying that everyone has 'equality of opportunity'. The latter embraces so many meanings, including 'we will not discriminate against you on the grounds of race, creed, colour, or gender because we don't want to or we're not allowed to'. So many tribunal cases exist today due to this misunderstanding that we are all the same and the conflict to which this inevitably leads. Is it time to look at conflict management in a new way? By focusing on how people are different rather than how similar they are? Would this enable us to make a distinction between the differences and work out what skills different people bring to the table? Could we begin to see that we are surrounded by everyday issues that could have positive outcomes beyond anything we thought possible?

Our assumptions are a useful shorthand

Sometimes, our assumptions are as useful to us as they are annoying or helpful to others. Marianne, who works with us, has been married for 37 years. Over lunch one day we were chatting about assumptions. It sort of started when she said that when I phone and ask her what's for lunch her assumption is that I am hungry. She's right, just like for 37 years she has assumed that her husband will get up and make her a cup of tea first thing in the morning. They have never really talked about this and it has become for her a very useful assumption. A far more annoying assumption for her is the one he has made for the last 37 years that the bills will, somehow by magic, get paid every month. Sometimes we know we hold an assumption and almost move it to the world of fact – if I drink four litres of water a day I will increase my general well-being.

We sometimes hear people saying: "Oh no, I can see the potential danger of assumptions that are wrong, I don't want to risk it, so I won't have any." As far as Partnering is concerned, this is not only impossible but undesirable. This, in itself, is an assumption!

Assumptions are an inevitable and useful shorthand for us. And we can choose any and every assumption we hold. As this is the very basis of Partnering, the word 'choice' suddenly takes on a more profound meaning. If we are responsible for our own assumptions that guide our actions, then we are responsible for bringing about the difference we want to see.

Partnering suggests that, if we are not making the difference we want to make, then perhaps we are not challenging our own assumptions. Questioning our own assumptions makes us realise that all other positions and stances taken by people are made on several assumptions. We come to realise that the differences between us are not so much our religion, culture, community spirit, company ethos, but the assumptions we take that lead us to hold such positions. The differences between us are differences in the assumptions we hold.

Discovering and naming the assumptions we hold

One of the most powerful Partnering meetings I have ever attended was at the launch of a new project. The project leader had gathered together all the key stakeholders for the project and included both senior people as well as those 'on the ground'. The group spent the day talking about the assumptions they were holding. At first, they really struggled to make a distinction between what they considered to be 'facts' and what they were prepared to identify as 'assumptions'. To help things along we suggested that everyone take a few moments and write up on the sheets around the room all the facts, so that we could get them out the way and discuss the assumptions. By the end of the day we were still having fascinating conversations about the facts. We had to allocate more time. With so many people complaining about all this chatter and the lack of action, how tight the deadlines were and how much time was being wasted, it was a difficult decision for the project manager to take.

That project is now consistently running below budget and ahead of the timetable. The speed with which people voice their assumptions (and work with the one person who is still holding fast to the fact that, as an engineer, he doesn't have assumptions, only facts) is tenfold payback for the one day invested up front. Next time you are in a meeting, agreeing on a project with new partners, talking to your customers about what they want, try naming a few assumptions and see what happens.

In any situation, if you want to make a difference, it is of value to notice and name your assumptions up front. Not only does it save time, it stops one less than useful assumption leading to another.

Discovering the assumptions we hold and do not notice

Even more startling than our reluctance to name the assumptions we know we hold, is how so many of us fail to notice the impact that our unconscious assumptions have on how we react. And this is not about subtle stuff but the most obvious.

One of the situations where my assumptions run riot is when my secretary calls me to tell me that a client wants to speak to me. Immediately, I am in panic mode – what have I done, what is wrong, what could the problem be? My heart races, I think about closing the business down, moving to an island. Yet I make the call and discover that they have won the contract we were helping them to land, sorted the dispute out that has plagued them for months etc. From my past experience as a kid, whenever anyone 'wanted to talk to me' there was only one purpose – I was in trouble. No matter how old we get, our TICing models will be influenced by the historical assumptions we hold. In these contexts holding our assumptions lightly is the only way to discover the purpose of the call.

We often assume 'fact' so don't question the meaning. In so doing, we take an assumption into the next situation that may not be very useful. Then, when our assumption is challenged, we may not respond in a positive way, depending on what is influencing us at that time.

Can we afford to build layer upon layer of assumptions in this way? Wouldn't we all take a way out of this if it was fairly simple and straightforward?

In mediation there is often an assumption that someone crying is 'upset'. Crying is often a result of something else – frustration or anger. It's useful to ask rather than assume, in order to be able to 'see' the other person in the mediation. 'Oh, I assumed you were upset.'

We all make assumptions that turn out to be less than useful. I entered a room full of people to lead a workshop. My eyes fixed upon a guy looking like a misery guts in the corner. When we went through the early important exercise of checking out what people's objectives were and learning something of the attitudes they were bringing into the room, it turned out that this guy has panic attacks when he is in a room with no windows. There is a simple way to learn how to strip off the layers of assumptions – just ask.

What can we do about our assumptions?

Far from a desperate situation, this is something common to all of us. We all make assumptions that are useful and useless. The key is to learn to bring to the surface all our assumptions in a way that best enables a successful outcome: pay attention to the thinking in your head and the language you use to express it. That is, assume good intent.

We need to get into the right kind of conversations to enable things to be different. This invites the question, 'Is there a right and wrong kind of conversation?' If we are committed to adopting a Partnering ethos, we come to see that enabling the right kind of conversation to take place is all about our determination to have a 'different' kind of conversation in which we make our assumptions explicit and ensure that they are 'heard'. This can enable two organisations in conflict to have a conversation that changes everything completely. Remember those two organisations in Chapter 1 who had been in conflict for 20 years and they sorted it out in one day? Well, the key solution was to help them to see that divorce was the best outcome. A different kind of conversation freed them to see a different kind of relationship and move to produce better things.

There is no prescription for the right kind of conversation. On the other hand, one of the best things we can be doing is to notice the brilliant conversations we have, wherever they are and whatever they're like. It starts with noticing what is effective in the way we currently communicate.

There are some things in the way we currently communicate that are really effective. My guess is that most people don't know when they're communicating effectively. People only know when they're getting it wrong.

Can you remember the last time you had a brilliant conversation?

Next time you have one, you may begin to learn a great deal about your own assumptions and those of others in conversations that create possibility and give life.

Partnering is only effective when it recognises the point of view of the 'other' partner. How else are we going to do this unless we make our individual and collective assumptions explicit? Doing so is a great way of recognising the differences and understanding how they will inform how we need to work together. It takes imagination. Then again, 'everything is possible' is an imaginative assumption to hold.

Exploring our Partnering assumptions

As much as we're telling people there is no model for Partnering, we know that it's a good idea to begin every Partnering relationship with a set of assumptions that can influence a positive outcome. If we're Partnering effectively, we may not know what a positive outcome is until we discover it together. As we've seen from experience, every situation offers us the possibility of benefiting from a Partnering ethos; however, we can name seven Partnering assumptions we have found useful in a range of contexts. The accompanying examples show the benefit of starting out with these assumptions.

Seven useful Partnering assumptions

Conflict is a great natural resource

We hold appreciation, good will and good intent

There are multiple realities and we choose what becomes our truth

In every situation we find what is working and learn from it

The questions we ask determine the direction we take

The language we use creates our world

Trust emerges through the integrity of our conversations

Seven useful Partnering assumptions

As we explore these assumptions I wonder what the example is in your mind right now? What is the situation you are facing where just one or two of these assumptions could help you to move the situation on, resolve a 20-year conflict, increase your profits, deliver exceptional service to the public? Or simply sort out something that has niggled at you for months?

1 Conflict is a great natural resource

There is some logic in selecting this as the first of the Partnering assumptions. As we explore in greater depth in the next chapter, to partner is to have conflict. Nature provides one of the greatest examples of Partnering. Look at most of the coastlines of our countries and you will see fascinating, unique and complex rock formations. This has come about due to the conflict of the waves and sand coming into conflict with the rock.

When working in organisations, we often find one of the assumptions that frees people to think differently is when we propose they hold an assumption that conflict is a great natural resource. They do not have to make it up, engineer it, set out a strategy to ensure it happens – it just is. Partnering means everything becomes possible, yet Partnering can fail if people do not understand how to behave in ways that generate trust and lay the foundations to meet conflict and challenge *affirmatively*.

I see that most attempts at Partnering fail because the assumption is that when there is conflict this is somehow always bad, an indication of a lack of trust at best or worse, getting into the 'agree to disagree' mode. However, if my starting assumption is that conflict is a great natural resource, then when it happens I am ready. For one simple reason – I absolutely know that great things can come of this. Pop into Chapter 5 now if you want to explore this assumption in more depth.

Before you go, just think about a conflict or difference you are currently dealing with at work. It could be a difference between two individuals, between your organisation and a key supplier or between two divisions in the same company. Just how much energy, time and resource are going into managing around it – and how would it be different if you asked everyone involved to assume 'they had the resource for just one week'.

2 We hold appreciation, good will and good intent

Assumptions are choices – when Partnering we can choose to hold appreciation, good will and good intent as our starting point. Not necessarily as a one-off, but rather in every conversation and interaction. This assumption becomes easier if we are holding that conflict is a natural resource, as it increases our capacity to think about the differences others bring in a way to get the best from them.

For me, there are two ways in which this assumption can prove useful. The first is when, due to the relationships I establish and the general assumptions I hold about the people around me, I have decided I will assume this position. I have found that more often than not, if I get over myself and understand what has happened, then the decisions people take, the actions they take and the way they behave are things I can work with.

The other way I find it useful is when my logic (which after all could just be a collection of assumptions), my gut and everything else scream something at me – namely, that, in this situation I can absolutely not assume appreciation, good will and good intent, so I half assume them between gritted teeth. Then, what I find is that people start acting with appreciation, good will and good intent, despite themselves. In my personal relationships, I find holding this assumption to be one of the most useful and at times most difficult to hold.

One day I allowed myself to think the unthinkable. I'm a person known for valuing the differences in others, yet a thought snuck into my head – how come I am the only man on the planet whose partner doesn't just occasionally help me by putting my clothes away? Now before you leap up convinced of my Neanderthal tendencies, assuming that I am sexist beyond redemption – I did say it was a thought that snuck into my head and it happens occasionally. So, on this day I decided to understand my partner's logic. Was it simply that I was big and ugly enough to do it myself? In my view, a very reasonable assumption. Her answer was simple. "You know, we were laughing at the fact that my father had a hard time in our house with two girls and my mother. Because until my sister and I started having boyfriends we did not realise that men look for things with men's eyes. You say, 'Darling, it's not here!' when we know it's right under your nose. So, I knew that if I put anything away you would wander around never being able to find it."

In business it is perhaps more challenging to hold this assumption of good will and intent. I find that in my work I travel extensively. There can often be weeks before I see the team in the office. The funny thing is that the longer I travel the more difficult it is to hold this assumption in relation to my own colleagues. I begin to imagine all kinds of reasons lying behind the actions that are being taken. The moment we sit down in the green kitchen for one of Marianne's famous lunches then the assumption is easy to hold again. The more global our business dealings become and the more we rely on remote working, the more we dehumanise each other – and the more we need to hold this assumption about appreciation, good will and good intent.

3 There are multiple realities and we choose what becomes our truth

As I am sure you will notice, this assumption builds on the notions we explored in the previous chapter on what we notice and how we increase our capacity to notice different things. If a team which is Partnering to deliver a major project holds this assumption then what becomes different? The most significant thing is that people will be awake and alive to the notion that, when coming out of a critical meeting about deadlines and penalty clauses, there will be a multitude of realities for the people involved. And that, mostly for good reason, people will come to understand their truth – which is often different to that of their colleagues.

This assumption is useful as it helps us to see that, while acknowledging the multiple realities that exist, we have the choice as individuals and partners to decide which truth we will hold.

In pan-African events like the one in Ghana, there is one exercise that is very powerful for people – it is called the 'wall of greatness'. The vision of the programme is to work towards transforming Africa from the begging bowl to the continent of majesty. Each person on the programme is invited to bring three paper bricks on which they put the things they are most proud of in their countries. During an electric afternoon we go through a process of discussing these strengths and then building the wall of greatness. At one of the events, having built the wall and taken some time for reflection, an old woman stood weeping and said: "For the first time in my life I realise that we in Africa have everything we need to transform ourselves – it is the way that we as people use and manage what we have that results in a begging bowl reality. And people can change, therefore we can change a continent."

What is the reality you are creating in your organisation?

Graeme went to the 'Customer service' hutch at his local railway station. He asked for a feedback form and was given a complaints form. "No, I want to feedback something good," he told the railway official. He had been given great service and, holding a principle of appreciation, wanted to tell the people responsible.

It turned out that there was no other form, so he had to cross out 'complaints' and hand it in with his praise. One week later he got a letter from the station manager – "thanks, really appreciated, we don't get thanked very often". This wasn't surprising, as the system was only set up with the reality that people would be complaining – and, as Graeme had noticed, there are multiple realities about the rail staff.

In your organisation you may want to turn your attention to exploring the realities you have created as truth. If 'everyone' believes that the sole purpose of the finance department is to make life difficult for people then the more you focus on that the more it becomes a truth within the organisation.

4 In every situation we find what is working and learn from it
This assumption is profoundly different to the assumption that we learn from our mistakes. I am not suggesting for one minute that we do not – once we get over the feelings of failure, hopelessness, anger at ourselves, irritation at the stupidity of others – then absolutely we learn a lot from the mistakes we make. There are so many reasons why we are so good at learning from what has not worked. Mostly it is because we are just so good at remembering the detail of when we have made a mistake.

Seven years ago I worked with a group for one day, and for 20 seconds after lunch I verbally assaulted someone who was biologically attached to his mobile telephone in an inappropriate way. It was a mistake that I instantly regretted and I can still remember the shirt he had on (bad) and the room we were in (stuffy). That one regret instantly assumed a greater power and proportion than the many successes we had achieved as a small business, setting off with £1,000 capital and growing 400% per year.

How many organisations do you see setting up a project team to analyse what happens when a project fails? And yet, when there has been a success, we move swiftly onto the next thing coming our way.

There is no way that we can ever hope to learn from what is working if we fail to even notice it, let alone understand the detail that stands behind it. We work with a simple technique that has come to be called StarFish. In this simple process, two people engage in a conversation for about 30 minutes guided by questions that are affirmatively disruptive. StarFish engages everyone in the organisation in a way that focuses attention on what they are doing well and what it is that helps them to do that.

It is neither easy nor natural for most of us to learn from what is working. However, the energy, trust and passion that are formed when partners take the time to discuss and understand what is working allow them to set up a savings account of this data. Then, when conflict abounds, trust is low and people are choosing a truth of dysfunction, they can draw from the collective memory of what works, rather than relying on credit.

One of the leaders we worked with a few years ago told us a great story after one of the sessions when we had worked with this assumption. His son had been in the school football team since he was seven. He was now nine and over the last two years their team had never won a single game. As he described it, he had now really drawn the short straw and was appointed as the team coach. That night he had gone to one of their matches and thought, well nothing else has worked so I might as well try this. At half time they were, as usual, 3-0 down. He spoke to them and, digging really deep, he managed to identify at least one thing that each of the team had done in the first half that could be described as something that had worked. That night they won 9-3.

Think about the way in which many organisations receive feedback from their customers – how much of the information focuses on what is really working for people?

This question leads us to reflect on the next of our assumptions.

5 The questions we ask determine the direction we take

I am amazed at some of the things that organisations continue to do without seeming to think about the impact that this has on their employees or customers. Do you understand the logic of an employee survey that leads to people thinking the place they work in is terrible, they hate their job, there are no development opportunities... and it is all someone else's fault?

It is a bit like going to a group of really satisfied customers to understand what we could be doing better and driving them to think about the times when we have not delivered what we should have. We leave them once again focused on poor service.

I am reminded of an occasion when the leader of a large American organisation I was working with approached me at the end of an excellent day and simply asked – what has disappointed you in this process? In an instant my mind had shifted from what was possible to what was not. Now, from my experience of him, I knew there was good intent in his question. He is a very dynamic man who is sure to go far in his career. We have been impressed by the speed with which he is working with the ethos of Partnering and guiding his organisation through a significant change process. We have come to rely on his capacity to work in a powerful and positive way. At one point in their change programme we had just completed a very successful training workshop for 60 internal change agents. We had started with a very sceptical group and, working with my colleagues from Nigeria, Ethiopia and Ghana, the group had significantly moved on in their thinking and use of the Partnering tools. It was amazing to see American engineers challenged by and learning from this African team. Yet I was still amazed that he should focus his powerful question on what had not worked.

As a leader, one of society's decision-makers, what direction do you take your world in?

Given the strength and power that questions hold, we have chosen to focus on this area in more depth in Chapter 5. The art of questioning is something that, once you begin to discover it, will engage and fascinate you endlessly. Try noticing the questions that are asked around you and the impact they have.

6 The language we use creates our world

I'm so reminded of the eloquence of Marie Fatayi-Williams, the Nigerian mother whose son was killed in the London bombings of 2005, and the newspaper reports about how powerful she was. One supportive journalist said that words should be worthy of the feelings that inspire them. We don't have to be Martin Luther King, Winston Churchill or Nelson Mandela to do that. In the way Marie put her language together, she allowed passion to come through when she spoke at the scene of the bus bombing. I am honoured to reproduce most of her words here.

"This is Anthony, Anthony Fatayi-Williams, 26 years old, he's missing and we fear that he was in the bus explosion... on Thursday. Now New York, now Madrid, now London. There has been widespread slaughter of innocent people. There have been streams of tears, innocent tears. There have been rivers of blood, innocent blood. Death in the morning, people going to find their livelihood, death in the noontime on the highways and streets.

"They are not warriors. Which cause has been served? Certainly not the cause of God, not the cause of Allah because God Almighty only gives life and is full of mercy. Anyone who has been misled, or is being misled to believe that by killing innocent people he or she is serving God

should think again because it's not true. Terrorism is not the way, terrorism is not the way. It doesn't beget peace. We can't deliver peace by terrorism, never can we deliver peace by killing people. Throughout history, those people who have changed the world have done so without violence, they have [won] people to their cause through peaceful protest. Nelson Mandela, Martin Luther King, Mahatma Gandhi, their discipline, their self-sacrifice, their conviction made people turn towards them, to follow them. What inspiration can senseless slaughter provide? Death and destruction of young people in their prime as well as old and helpless can never be the foundations for building society.

"My son Anthony is my first son, my only son, the head of my family. In African society, we hold on to sons. He has dreams and hopes and I, his mother, must fight to protect them. This is now the fifth day, five days on, and we are waiting to know what happened to him and I, his mother, I need to know what happened to Anthony. His young sisters need to know what happened, his uncles and aunties need to know what happened to Anthony, his father needs to know what happened to Anthony. Millions of my friends back home in Nigeria need to know what happened to Anthony. His friends surrounding me here… need to know what has happened to Anthony. I need to know, I want to protect him. I'm his mother, I will fight till I die to protect him. To protect his values and to protect his memory.

"Innocent blood will always cry to God Almighty for reparation. How much blood must be spilled? How many tears shall we cry? How many mothers' hearts must be maimed? My heart is maimed. I pray I will see my son, Anthony. Why? I need to know, Anthony needs to know, Anthony needs to know, so do many others unaccounted for innocent victims, they need to know.

"It's time to stop and think. We cannot live in fear because we are surrounded by hatred. Look around us today. Anthony is a Nigerian, born in London, worked in London, he is a world citizen. Here today we have Christians, Muslims, Jews, Sikhs, Hindus, all of us united in love for Anthony. Hatred begets only hatred. It is time to stop this vicious cycle of killing. We must all stand together, for our common humanity. I need to know what happened to my Anthony. He's the love of my life. My first son, my first son, 26. He tells me one day, 'Mummy, I don't want to die, I don't want to die. I want to live, I want to take care of you, I will do great things for you, I will look after you, you will see what I will achieve for you. I will make you happy.' And he was making me happy. I am proud of him, I am still very proud of him but I need to know where he is, I need to know what happened to him. I grieve, I am sad, I am distraught, I am destroyed… Where is he, someone tell me, where is he?"

This, we cannot forget once we have heard or read it. It's hard to follow with any comment or example that does not sound mundane. Language, however, is mainly for everyday use, stringing one mundane element together with another as we get on with our lives. This power of language is so familiar to us that we don't even notice it. When we do, we almost immediately forget it again. I was struck by the simple power of language when I got onto a British Midlands flight one day and the air crew made the following announcement: "Good afternoon, ladies and gentlemen. I would like to remind you that you are free to use your mobile telephones until we close the cabin doors." I have used that in workshops ever since. "Remember to turn your mobile phone on during the break to get your messages" has a different impact from"Turn your phones off!"

We drew previously on the example of the organisation that used the language of commands and war to describe the people in their teams.

What is the language that surrounds and supports you? How are you using language when you talk about and describe the people around you?

I worked with a manager in the voluntary sector who said it was all very well talking about leadership and stuff, but some people were beyond help. She explained that her administrator, Alice, was known as the Poisoned Chalice. Alice had been with the organisation for seven years yet got shunted to a different team every year or so because she never did her job properly and nobody had ever gone through the disciplinary process to get her out. This manager said she was now going to do that because it had to stop and Alice had to go.

We chatted about the impact of using a label like 'Poisoned Chalice'. Did that create a reality where it was difficult for her to change? If the manager and others brought appreciation, good will and good intent to Alice's situation, how might that have a different effect?

We met again at a conference. I asked how it was going and she said that people in her office could not believe what had happened. It was time for Alice's appraisal. Now Alice knew from experience that 'appraisal' meant getting told off, so she was ready – arms crossed, shoulders hunched. The manager started the meeting by saying: "Thank you. I just wanted you to know that two weeks ago last Tuesday the management team had a really productive meeting. Everyone was well prepared and that enabled us to have some great discussions and take some positive decisions. Because you had planned the meeting, got the papers out on time and ensured we all knew where we were going, you helped us to prepare and do a good job. I appreciate that."

Alice's shoulders slowly drooped in astonishment at this unexpected turn of events. This was not supposed to happen. The manager continued. "Your role is important and it is important you keep that standard up. I have to say, this is not always the case. There have been other management meetings where you have not been able to prepare in this way. I am curious, what is it that has prevented you from doing the great job that we know you are capable of on these other occasions? What could we do differently to help you reach the high standards that you can achieve?"

And then they had an open, constructive and honest conversation – about some of the challenges at home, some things that would help, the fact that Alice thought nobody noticed or cared how she did her job and that she assumed she had been written off, so what was the point?

My manager friend said Alice's performance since has been exemplary and it's like having a new friend in the office. Of course, other people say 'it will never last' – and their scepticism puts a burden on her. They limit her with their disbelief, but the manager says she has seen the power of helping people to recognise, and build on, what they do well, and the importance of the language we use to label people.

7 Trust emerges through the integrity of our conversations

When thinking about Partnering particularly in the context of business or organisational relationships, I think the notion of trust is an interesting one. Somehow we have come to see trust as something that is static – an either/or, I trust you or I don't. With much pride and arrogance we are sometimes heard to say things like: "It takes a lot to earn my trust." "Once you have lost my trust you will never regain it." "You should never trust them."

Have we completely lost our senses? As there is good logic for me in starting our seven assumptions with conflict, there is equally good logic in ending our assumptions with trust. If you were to hold every one of the assumptions we have discussed in this section then it becomes inevitable that we see trust as something that is constantly moving and in flux. If I hold appreciation and discover what lay behind a decision you made that I disagreed with then I have in that same moment moved from starting to question or mistrust you to realising that my reality was not the only truth.

I can equally question you in a way that reinforces trust or starts to break it down and destroy it. How could our relationships and interactions be different if what we trust is that people notice things in different ways, that we hold assumptions that we have the capacity to change and adjust, that conflict is a natural resource and when managed well produces the most amazing outcomes?

Trust emerges through the conversations we have, the courage we muster, our attempts to engage in understanding our different realities, our conversations that grapple with the conflicts that erupt. We need to stay in constant conversation with our partners, understanding on an immediate level their TICing models and on a broader level their shifting understandings, priorities and pressures. Recognise that the notion of trust as a static, once-lost-never-regained state of being is too simplistic for human interaction.

I find difficulty enough trusting myself – to go to the gym in the morning, to keep to my resolution not to drink too much beer – to hold an assumption of appreciation, good will and good intent when I am stuck in the depths of an automated telephone system.

Working with these assumptions?

What are some of the ways in which you could very quickly and easily work with these assumptions?

A quick and simple strategy would be to take a copy of this list of assumptions and discuss them in the team or when next you meet your customer or an important stakeholder. You will be amazed about how much you learn about all the other assumptions they hold, what they notice and what makes them TIC, simply by having this conversation.

Who should you be having a different conversation with?

You could try agreeing with your team that you will pick one assumption a week and everyone will hold it. What are you noticing about what is different? What can you learn from this?

You may find that the most useful thing to do is to discuss the notion of assumptions with your customer and then agree on the assumptions that best work for you in the language that will make the most sense to your people.

Whatever you decide, you will start to notice the power you have over the assumptions you hold about the differences in other people and in your conflicts with those differences.

5

Partnering Conflict

Partnering helps us welcome differences and embrace conflict

Profit from the inevitable!

To partner is to have conflict. Anyone who has a close personal relationship will recognise and have personal experience of holding this assumption. If we see Partnering as the organisational DNA of the future, we will undoubtedly exceed our expectations of what is possible – so long as we take a gigantic leap in our ability to exploit differences and manage conflict in a way that harnesses the profits and chops the costs immediately. Partnering requires Olympic-standard conflict management techniques and strategies.

I only have to mention the word 'conflict' for everyone to declare that, in this organisation, community, partnership, household, there is no conflict. Well, fair enough! Then they add, 'We do have disagreements, get a bit frustrated, cool down our communications for a few days, take a bit of time off, forget to pass on information, agree to put it behind us etc'. Only for it to bite them back at 2am. Yet, 'We have a good relationship, you see, because we avoid conflict.' And, 'We don't really want to call it conflict because that's serious, people would get hurt, collective interests would not be taken into account, powerful leaders would abuse their positions.' And so it goes.

My all-time favourite is, when working with this team in which there is no conflict, I am reassuringly told during the tea break that I simply do not understand the humour of the culture. Trouble is, I'm struggling to believe the evidence of my eyes and ears – seeing the verbal daggers flying across the board room table, in disputes and arguments that keep going around with the same players holding the same positions, coming to the same conclusions. And this is still not conflict? And this is how large corporations are led?!

There is good reason for our reluctance to open the can of words – we feel that we lack the skills or tools to 'sort it out' and we don't want to make it worse. The only strategy we do know about is good old humour. I was working with an executive team who could not have found a bigger table to spread themselves around and be further from each other. The fact that a number of 'pairs' were closer to each other and the leader had his own 'section' of the table were something else. Some of the things that happened you may well recognise. It started while one person was talking. Across the room one of the pairs began whispering, sharing a warm smile, a raised eyebrow. As the speaker droned on with no end in sight a comment was lobbed across the table. Cue some sharp intakes of breath, then, in quick succession, a few giggles, a "Well it's true" and a "Come on, we have to be able to laugh", soon moving to a "No offence, it's a joke" and finally a "Phew! It's tea time and I just have to make this phone call."

Hmm… A little bit of sarcasm here, a funny one-liner that draws a laugh over there. 'They're just words!' I can't deny they're words, but 'just' words? Not in any definition of 'just' I can find. To me, they were far from 'just'. Using humour in a situation of real conflict only leaves the issue in nuance and people do not actually get it. People walk out of the room feeling something's resolved, only to find some of the aspects of the conflict are entrenched, by being 'named', often in a humorous way. We're back in the jungle of the school playground, where children apply nicknames to other children and staff, purely as a coping mechanism. 'There's something about that person I don't like or don't understand. I'll deal with it by naming a personality trait.'

CAN OF WORDS – MANAGEMENT SPEAK

Another way we deal with conflict is to disguise it in words. Although we've named it – it's called 'management speak' – do we know when we're indulging in it ourselves? After all, we allow ourselves to write people off very quickly because of the jargon they're using. One of the best ways to silence anyone in organisations is to accuse them of management speak. In other words, until you can talk to me in my language (the right language), I will just exclude you. In many organisations, however, we can see that people have developed very useful ways of talking with each other. They develop a familiarity. Now, within half an hour of meeting with some clients, we hear this: "You guys sound like you have worked with our organisation your whole life." We have come to realise over time that they're telling us this simply because we are paying attention in that context to the words they're using. Not only that, but how they're using them, the meaning they're giving to them and what energy they get behind them. Then, very quickly, we start to adopt and to use those words. It requires us to avoid being lazy and saying, "Well, that's just jargon", or "That's just management speak."

I wonder what decisions shareholders and investors would make if they were able to look beyond the Profit and Loss and see into the boardrooms and corridors of the companies they are investing in. They'd see school uniforms swapped for pin-striped suits. Would they also see that there was no conflict, that the time spent in petty politics, empire building, competing within the same organisation were all valuable ways for people to spend their time and the investors' money? Those who do see this often believe it to be an inevitable part of doing business. What is inevitable is the conflict. What is not inevitable is the loss we make as a result of not knowing how to deal with it.

If the language we use creates our world and we are brave enough to use the language of conflict when Partnering, we WILL do what it takes to profit from the difference.

As we briefly explored in the previous chapter, when we hold the assumptions that conflict is not only inevitable when we partner, but is also our greatest natural resource, we see the strength in working with the conflicts that arise to profit from them.

Re-defining the challenge

"Let's agree to disagree!" How many times have you heard this phrase? How many times have you uttered it?

Is it possible that this seemingly peace-making statement hides a multitude of sins? Get behind the words and what does it really mean?

If I say to you, "Let's agree to disagree," aren't I really saying, "You are wrong and I will get you to see the truth when you are feeling more reasonable"?

In which case, we have not really agreed anything and this issue will rise up again when it gets the chance.

There's nothing neutral or consensus-reaching about this statement. So, no, let's not agree to disagree – let's make the differences work for us. That sounds to me like a good place to start when we're talking about re-defining the challenge.

Do we assume that all conflicts seek solutions? When we hear the word 'conflict', perhaps our mind jumps to wars and violent power struggles. Every news bulletin features conflict in its most raw forms. Powerful winners, poor losers. It's hardly surprising, then, that when we examine our own lives we see no real conflict. Just a minor disagreement here, a misunderstanding there, nothing that can't be avoided for a quiet life, because life is too short.

Now, all my life experience tells me that life is too short NOT to deal with conflict. Conflict is everywhere. It may be avoidable (temporarily), but it is inevitable (ultimately). Trying to avoid conflict when you know it exists is no solution at all.

We need to pay careful attention to the language we use when we're dealing with conflict. Here's how we re-define the challenge:

Conflict is the process or method of *expressing* and/or acting out inevitable *disagreements* around personal, community or organisational outcomes, resources, products, services, systems or interactions which arise *due to differences* in assumptions, attitudes, values, priorities, lifestyles, perceptions and interests.

The big implication? If we think we know what conflict is, then we must have a way of managing it.

Conflict management is the strategy used by individuals, communities and organisations to *identify* and manage differences in order to *reduce* the human and financial costs of unmanaged conflict and *harness* conflict as a source of change, innovation and improvement.

Counting the cost – questions of indifference?

The costs to organisations who are partnering and not addressing the conflict are significant – failed projects, significant budget overspend, public inquiries etc. Put this together with the costs within organisations that are neither Partnering nor addressing conflict and we can quickly see these costs could come close to the current global costs of war. Literally.

Think for a moment about the last time you had a significant difference with someone. It could be you are in conflict with someone right now. Think about the amount of brain space you give it, the schemes you come up with in your head to seek retribution, the time you spend in conversations with others, justifying your position, embedding your assumptions as fact. Do you give as much time and energy to creating something?

Let's look for a moment at the costs within organisations of not embracing conflict.

What would it take for you to see well-managed conflict as a valuable investment with pay-off on the bottom line as well as in higher motivation for everyone involved?

Questions of indifference? I hardly think so.

You're probably aware of the costs incurred due to formal disputes – in legal fees, in employees' and managers' time administering grievances and complaints. Not forgetting the costs of bringing in external companies to arbitrate.

As far back as 1985, the legal expenses alone of corporations in the USA amounted to over 50 billion dollars – four times higher than in 1975. Today, they're much higher. There were more than 115,000 employment tribunal applications in the UK in 2004 – a rise of 17% on the previous year. Many legal firms now actively tout for compensation business – a sure sign that conflict is everywhere and there's money to be made from it!

In a survey conducted by the UK Department of Trade and Industry, three-quarters of employers are worried about the financial cost of tribunals. In 2003, 35% of 100,000 tribunal applications might have been avoided if appropriate discussions had taken place beforehand.

You can't afford it

No organisation can afford wasted management time, large tribunal awards, unlimited fines, legal fees and the inevitable damage to reputation, both internally and externally.

The legal fees and other expenses in settling formal disputes probably represent less than 10% of the total cost of conflict to an organisation.

How much could your organisation expect to save by strategically managing its informal conflicts?

Some in the field of conflict management would argue that this figure would sit anywhere between 10% and 50% of the total annual turnover.

Conflict costs employers time, money, employee commitment and reputation. And these are just the costs within an organisation. It costs individuals time, money and health and often impacts on personal relationships outside the work place. You can't afford it. Your people can't afford it. And it goes much wider than that. We only have to refer to the weekend papers to see endless examples of the costs to society when we fail to manage the conflicts between partners. Strikes bringing cities to a standstill, projects over-running by millions, delays to key services due to conflict about the purpose of the job. If society can't afford it, nobody can afford it.

How can we prevent the cost of conflict disabling our organisations and the individuals who comprise them and our wider communities?

The myth of conflict resolution

It seems obvious that, to avoid the spiralling costs of unmanaged conflict between individuals or corporations, conflict management techniques have to change. But how?

Several business models have identified the need to look at how people resolve conflict within organisations. If, despite their best efforts, they are struggling to achieve their aims, is it because they see conflict as something to be *resolved once and for all?*

If we begin to examine informal conflict a bit more closely, would it be possible for us to see that 'expressing disagreements due to differences' is an inevitable and permanent part of our social and working lives and, therefore, something we ought to use and keep using to our mutual advantage?

Telling people that they need to change their whole way of thinking is not normally conducive to change. It tends to bring out the cynic in all of us. All of a sudden you're back in that school scenario, standing in the Head's office. No matter how hard you try to concentrate on the rollicking of your life, there's nothing quite as fascinating as the silver hairs creeping out of the old man's nostrils.

Partnering avoids such pitfalls in organisations. It recognises that organisations are involved in increasingly more rapid change and bigger, more diverse and more complex projects. This means one thing: there are more and more differences between more and more different people.

Major contracts will increasingly aspire to adopt this approach. One of the greatest certainties is that most of the people in these organisations will not want it as it requires them to change, as individuals, towards collective goals. Partnering challenges people at all levels of an organisation. It redefines the nature of relationships.

The question then becomes: How do we react to other ways of thinking, acting and being? Fear or possibility?

If we begin by regarding these other ways as problems and issues, our way of thinking will be about conflict management, control systems, keeping fear of the future to a minimum. If we begin by seeing these other ways as positions of difference we can learn from, our way of thinking will be about exploiting that difference, minimising control, exploring how we work together, the art of the possible.

Let's be clear that seeing others' differences as the source of our development will challenge us way beyond the current aspiration of valuing and respecting the differences. Even getting this far has been a long path for many people in many organisations and cultures. It is not far enough. In many cases it has failed because people can see no reason to value and respect the differences in others.

Harness the power of conflict

If we are to harness the power and potential that conflict brings when we partner either individually, within a team or between organisations and nations, we need to start by exploring our understanding of difference. Our personal relationship, if you like, with difference.

I am reminded of my first trip to Nigeria and arriving at Lagos airport. I am often referred to in Africa as being of 'presidential' height after the former President of Zambia. By the time I got into the car that came to collect me I was working hard to be curious about the different approach to queuing. Having lived in the UK over the last few years, I am now well schooled in the art of queuing. You know you have it bad when, as an African, you start to challenge people who are not keeping to the queue.

That night, as we sat outside in the humid, noisy, unique bustle that is Lagos, I chatted to my friends Christine and Umar about this experience. In her wonderfully Nigerian way, Christine chuckled and said: "Why you so slow?" In Nigeria, the strength is in your ability to find your way to the front and get on. What is the point in waiting for life to pass you by?

Suddenly, I saw again that, by really understanding what lay behind the difference, I could appreciate and enjoy and learn from that difference. Lagos has become a wonderful opportunity for me to express another part of myself; oh, and to remember that difference is also about paying attention to the context – so I have not tried this approach at London Heathrow.

In the organisation in which I work and the community in which I live, if I am unable to start from an assumption that other people hold assumptions that are different to mine, then I significantly limit my ability to learn, understand, develop, have fun, be fascinated and profit.

How do you react to difference?

People have differences and there are all sorts of strategies for dealing with that knowledge – avoidance, silence, too much information, misinformation, disinformation, papering over the cracks, war. What is the right strategy for your organisation or community? The answer depends on how much people within it can cherish difference and work with it. This means opening people up to the idea of risk and discovering what it means to them. When people are trying to find a different path, most focus on the things that don't work very well.

What would happen for your organisation or community if people in it began to see the differences in others as the most exciting opportunity to bring about their own development?

If we see conflict as an inevitable expression of the differences between people or partners, then it becomes impossible to eliminate it. Not only impossible, but undesirable.

If we hold an assumption that conflict is one of our greatest natural resources we get beyond simplistic ideas of fight or flight and can draw on it as a source of great benefit. What could the beneficial outcomes be? Enabling people to express and understand the differences that are being made explicit in the conflict; working towards future possibilities for all.

I had the privilege of working with a leader in a public sector organisation who was one of the true masters of managing differences. The task we had was to lead and facilitate close to 40 organisations in the design, management and running of a major global Ministers' Conference. To make things more complex, for the first time, in addition to the Ministers' Conference and Parallel Symposium of Professionals, we were to welcome a total of 250 young people from each minister's country in a Youth Conference to give voice to the views of young people.

The meetings of the stakeholder groups were unbelievable. There could be upward of 50 people at any one meeting. Decisions would be taken, views expressed, minutes taken and actions agreed. As soon as the meeting was over, the 'real' work began. People would renegotiate what was agreed, think that an issue had not been raised when it was on the agenda for two hours, be clear that their view had not been heard. By the time people had reached their offices and consulted their senior colleagues, they would change the agenda once again. The objectives would shift and yet more side negotiations and meetings would take place.

The night before the Conference began the leader insisted that the key partners meet. They thought he was being ridiculous, wasting time, they had better things to do. And again we went through each minute of the days ahead of us only to find differences in almost every key event of the Conference.

It was one of the most successful conferences of its kind. The final event was brought to a close and a young woman stood on the stage talking to over 500 people, including ministers: "You are our mothers and our fathers," she said. "We cannot achieve the future without you, and you cannot achieve it without us." I began to reflect on what had made it a success. Quite simply, it was the relentless focus on the differences – understanding them, talking them through, recognising that resolution and sameness would not achieve the ends – added to the leader's own relentless focus on holding an assumption of good will and good intent that saw us through and resulted in a commitment by ministers to always include young people in their decisions.

Rather than 'resolve' the conflict, or nip it in the bud, we used techniques that helped the group to recognise it, question their assumptions and turn it into a positive outcome they could take into the future.

Working with conflict – drawing down the profits

We have spent much of this chapter challenging how partners think about conflict - the meaning we give to it, the emotions we attach to it, the assumptions that drive us and how we try and work with it. Now we're going to look at how we can work with conflict, exploring the process from starting to recognise it to creating profitable possibilities from it.

Step 1 – Could you think differently?

The most obvious place to start when you're considering strengthening your conflict management skills is with how you think, personally, as an individual. As Partnering asks us to acquire an attitude of curiosity that embraces differences in others, we are presented with a great personal challenge, as individuals, before we even get to discuss the conflict around us with others.

I wonder what situations you find yourself in right now?

Could you apply the principle of holding good will and intent in *your* conflict context, in *your* reality?

Perhaps it may be useful for you to think about what your primary assumption in that situation is? If that was suddenly whisked away and you saw absolute proof the assumption was incorrect - where would that leave you in the dispute?

Just because you're not at war does not mean there is no conflict in your life. Could you learn to recognise your humanity in the choices you're making in areas of your life you call anything but 'conflict'? We're not letting you off the hook – we wouldn't want you to stay in that place where you are not dealing with the issues!

Is it time for you to look at conflict and conflict management in a new way? By focusing on how people are different rather than how similar they are? Would this enable you to make a distinction between the differences and work out what skills different people bring to the table? Could you begin to see that you are surrounded by everyday issues that could have positive outcomes beyond anything you thought possible?

Step 2 – Could you enable others to think differently?

When Partnering you need to create a safe environment where people can start to cash in on conflict, where they can notice the differences they see and what they call them. This will ensure that the people around can begin to think about and see conflict as a natural resource.

Conflict can arise in small ways, at short notice and settle quickly into myths that become truth for many people. If we see that the management of conflict is the management of differences between people, then we need to learn to recognise it and turn it to our advantage.

I was asked to work with a team that was seen as very dysfunctional by its manager and the rest of the organisation. In preparing for the event I had spoken to each member of the team. While I was learning a lot about what they did and the things that concerned them – reduction in budgets, poor office environment, new head office purchasing strategies – I was not getting much of an idea about what was disturbing this particular team. These were issues similar to those of other teams who seemed to work well together.

By lunch time on the first day I began to wonder whether the issues were ever going to surface. After lunch I did an exercise I have done many times. Called the 'conflict model', it helps individuals within a team situation to raise the issues they have in a way that encourages people to ask questions for understanding rather than justification. By the time we had all the issues out, the entire wall was covered with comments about the new purchasing procedures, long working hours etc. The group was fairly big and, as is common in these situations, some people got very actively engaged in organising the issues into themes while others look on. One of the particularly tall people in the group who was standing right at the back, pointed to an issue and told the person standing closest to it to move it somewhere else. As she moved to do as she was asked, she suddenly stopped, swung round and said, "That is just so typical of you – you stand about doing nothing while the rest of us are run off our feet. Everyone complains about it, comments are passed all day and you just ignore us – I have had enough!"

Finally, I could relax. I knew that we were going to find a way for this team to work together. I calmly sat down, inviting everyone to take a seat so we could have a chat. We resolved that issue along with a number of other things that had been bubbling for some time. At the end of the day a number of the group told how tense they had been when their colleague made her outburst.

Step 3 – What assumptions are people noticing and naming?
Thinking about conflict differently provides us with a foundation for building and strengthening conflict management techniques. The challenges and opportunities available to organisations are immense. I have tried to focus on a few of the most instantly practical strategies and techniques that you can employ to start getting to grips with the conflicts around you.

Once you have got your mind around thinking differently about differences, the fun can really start. And I do mean fun – when you increase your ability to notice the differences around you and pay attention to how you and others are naming those differences, endless possibilities emerge.

One of the first things we notice is that people are making assumptions about how other people are thinking and behaving. When we create a safe environment for people to raise issues, it doesn't take long for people with obvious or hidden concerns with others to begin pointing out conflicting points of view they attribute to irreconcilable differences in personality. We have come to name this 'personality clash'. The funny thing with personality clashes is that it always seems to be the other person's personality that is clashing. Think for a moment what you might be noticing and how you and others are naming it when you talk with such careless ease of personality clashes. One of our common understandings is that, in the main, people's personalities do not change. We hold a number of assumptions about personalities: they're fixed, cannot change, are a result of nature, or nurture, or both. Short of performing some sort of lobotomy, we see no way of changing these assumptions.

So, what do we do? We move those people to different departments or areas of the organisation, the team puts up with the sniping and poor communications, the person is promoted so they become someone else's issue.

If we notice this clash as differences in assumptions, behaviours and realities, how does it change? Could there be less cause for right and wrong, could there be less need for resolution and more for fascination?

Step 4 – Are people being careful with the language they use?

Being careless with the language we use is most harmful when we are referring to situations of conflict or difference. We stand by and let people create a reality around the difference using language that entrenches and re-enforces the hopelessness of the situation. 'They are always like that... ', 'That's their hidden agenda... ', 'Never trust what they are saying... ', 'They will always work in silos... ', 'Management are clueless... ', 'You are either in or out... ', 'He's a chameleon... ', 'She's a bully', 'We are facing disaster.'
Give it a go – focus on what you are noticing about the differences you see, the language you use to describe it, how others are talking about it and reinforcing everyone's views. Now try on another day to see something in each difference that you know you could create something effective out of.

Step 5 – Are people seeing the difference between event and meaning?

What's in a truth? In conflict we are so very fond of getting to the truth: 'How thick was the plank he hit her with?', 'Yes, you did ignore me,' 'I wrote down exactly what you said, word for word.'

One of my favourite exercises when I am working with a group is to suddenly pick up a spare chair, return it to the ground and immediately ask 'What just happened?' Those who weren't concentrating tend to say there was a noise, that someone at their table seemed startled by something. Others will say I threw the chair down, or even slammed the chair down, or claim I was going to stand on the chair, or was expecting someone to come in and show us something as they sat on the chair. Someone might even tell me I was trying to wake my colleague Graeme up.

This simple exercise gives us a profound insight into the world of conflict within and between organisations. In our daily lives numerous events are occurring all the time. A chair is moved, someone misses a meeting, we get a promotion, secure a contract. These are all events – the key is the meaning that we and others give to that event.

A colleague of ours was living in a communal house with a couple. The couple decided to get their own house and moved out. The day after they left they phoned and said to my colleague: "We realise that we have forgotten our food in the fridge and freezer, stuff like curry sauce, chutney etc. Please use whatever is perishable and we will come and collect the rest in three weeks' time when we get back from holiday."

My colleague stormed into the office as soon as they put the phone down and sounded off about the mean-minded ******** etc. Six days later she was still angry about how mean and selfish the couple were. The meaning that she had given to the event was, to her, clear and a fact. For her, things like generosity were important, particularity when it came to food. In her culture, food in a communal home would never be owned. Therefore, she came to the conclusion that it showed how mean they were – and after all she had done to help them!

Recognising that my colleague did have a good relationship with the couple which was now being seriously threatened, and that we would all go mad in the office if we had to continue to hear this story, I made the following comment: "Given that you never cook and that there were always jokes in the house about the 'strange' food they made, being vegans, I wonder if they were worrying about the food going to waste rather than not wanting you to have it?" And I left it at that. A few days later we were back to normal. My colleague was complaining about the smell of the spices in the fridge interfering with the taste of her open bottle of wine and was looking forward to catching up with them again.

The point – when you are helping people to see the difference between an event and the meaning they give to it – is to drop a few different meanings into the conversation rather than trying to ram one different meaning down their throat, which would simply replace one false fact with another.

One of the key strategies that helps us to see the meaning we are giving to the events around us involves trying to find our primary assumption and knocking it down – where are you now?

If my primary assumption in business is that people have a hidden agenda then I am in for a tough time. I will spend endless hours trying to discover what it is, assign my team to do some investigating and hypothesising and, of course, when I still do not discover what it is I am even more convinced that there is one. If my assumption is that everyone has an outcome they want to achieve – that having a clear idea on the outcomes I want is normal, natural and good business – then, as a partner, I will work with you to understand the outcomes you want to achieve. And we call this a hidden agenda?!

Step 6 – Are people looking at the different levels of conflict?

Working on how we see or understand conflict, noticing differences and naming them in a different way, exploring the difference between events and meanings by toppling our primary assumptions – all are simple and at times difficult ways of working with conflict. All are strategies aimed at increasing our understanding of what is happening around us in a way that most enables us to profit from it.

A useful means of getting to grips with the inevitable differences that occur between people and groups is the MITS model. This is a powerful way of beginning to look at the different levels at which the conflict is 'owned'.

Me – what are the aspects of this conflict that are actually down to me, that hit my personal triggers or that will be best resolved by me? You will recall that, in Chapter 3, we talked about what is making us TIC. If I am prepared to be honest with myself, what are my issues, in this particular context, that have precious little to do with the current conflict or issues?

Individuals – here, we're looking at issues between individuals – between yourself and someone else or between two other people. Now, before you jump back to the laziness of the personality clash, remember that this is about the differences between individuals that can be understood and worked with. What could be making us TIC, what role are we playing and what responsibility could we take to make a difference?

Team or group – the issues and dynamics within the team or group must also be considered to understand the conflict that is happening. If people are working together collectively and not acknowledging their differences, how is this contributing?

System – and finally, we need to look at how the system within which people are operating contributes to the differences or conflict. How does the bonus system that rewards the individual contribute to the corporate value of teamwork?

What are the MITS contributions you see in the following story?

I was asked to conduct a mediation between two managers within a national organisation. I was told that the two people involved had some differences that just needed to be sorted out quickly so that their teams could get on with their work. Essentially this was seen as a conflict between Individuals.

As I began to talk with the two people involved I came to see how many things were impacting on the situation that had arisen between them. Far from being something that belonged to the individuals, this situation required a complete MITS view. One thing that was contributing the most to them not being able to resolve things was their collective sense of injustice that this issue was being seen as personal between the two of them. I have learnt that, when people feel a sense of injustice, you will never help them to move on unless you work on the level of MITS. Very few conflicts can be put down to clashes between individuals – if you do not look at it on all levels individuals will not be able to resolve their own issues.

In this instance, we did resolve the issues between the two individuals. Moving from the mediation context to working with the teams, we resolved the other issues there. What we did not resolve were the things within the organisation or system that had contributed to the dispute – as that required the organisation to get honest about what its structure and senior people contributed to the issues.

Some insight into the organisation's issues may give you an opportunity to think about the similarities in your organisation.

The organisation had won a contract, which required two divisions to work together. The company was organised into 10 divisions, all working independently. Two were considered as being larger, more important and more critical to the overall organisation. The leaders of these two divisions were known to have a personality clash and both had their sights on the Chief Executive post.

One of the managers, Sarah, came from a PR agency background. She had recently left the hectic agency world to join the national organisation and focus on one client. She was appalled at the lack of organisation, accountability and focus she saw within the organisation. The other manager, Louise, had been in the organisation for 25 years. As a proud Irish woman, she held a strong sense of nationalism. Louise had project responsibility for the members of the team who were running the project, whereas Sarah had line responsibility for four of the team members. Sarah's partner worked in the team and turned out to be having a very close relationship with one of the other team members!
I will not go on with all the details – you can see how a complex combination of personal, individual, team and system issues all come together to create the conflicts that we don't deal with. In the end, we did manage to help the team to deliver the project to meet the customers' requirements. The organisation itself, however, was not prepared to look at how its structure and the political fighting between senior leaders were contributing a significant amount of time when such resources were required to ensure the project was a success. As a result, we needed to facilitate a number of team meetings, conduct at least one mediation a month and help the team to put a range of processes in place to manage decision-making.

So we can see that while it is possible to make a success of these kinds of projects without changing things in the system that are unhelpful, had the organisation-changed some things it would have cost them and the people less in the long run.

The role of communication in conflict

Let's re-iterate where we've come so far: we've seen that conflict, as the expression of difference, is inevitable and that recognising its existence is the beginning of a path that could save millions; we've seen it's a myth to think we can resolve it once and for all and that the best possibility is to embrace it and work with it; we've looked at some settings for drawing out and working with assumptions. Now, let's take a big step back and look at the bigger picture – the world of human communication.

How many of us have had the sense that there are just some debates we can never have because to merely begin to discuss the subject would be to raise a taboo, in the sense that whoever expressed an opinion on either side could be labelled for life? This may call to mind some of the bigger things in life – the issues of gender, race, the right to life itself. Would the latter be a potential debate about 'abortion' or the 'right to life'? Who decides? How do you even begin to have the discussion? Yet, it can become a habit not to discuss anything at all, right down to the smallest things in life: conflict avoidance, as the ostrich said, shortly before sticking its head into the sand at the sight of a herd of wildebeest on the horizon.

'Saying something' is at the heart of working with the differences between people. Words. Communication. All organisations know this. We tell ourselves that communication is critical. And yet, despite all our good intent and channels of communication, so often people don't feel communicated with. We develop a communication strategy, and then don't refer to it. We have a communication team – and then don't involve them. There are too many meetings and they add too little value. We have internet access and e-mail for everyone. There is good intent. We copy all and sundry in so that they are 'informed', or to cover our backs. And the impact is that people are swamped and end up not reading. We end up e-mailing the person at the next desk. And people use the e-mail to say the things that they are not prepared to say in person. We hear people say: "Why didn't they tell us about this change?" When we enquire into the situation, we hear: "Yes, I got the six e-mails, I filled in the questionnaire, but they never communicated with me".

Understanding communication in conflict culture

I am often faced with an odd look when I ask people to think about their organisation's conflict culture. Given that they are still struggling to accept that there is conflict, I guess this is not surprising.

Let's look at conflict cultures. How are they created and how do they change? If we accept that organisational cultures are formed and created by the people within the organisation then our starting point needs to be understanding what different individuals bring into the organisation. Much of our conflict culture is informed by our own histories with conflict or difference.

How was conflict managed in your home when you were growing up? How differently or similarly is conflict expressed now in your own home?

Some of us repeat the methods we learnt in childhood, others work really hard NOT to repeat those lessons. As adults, when we make a home with someone else we each bring our own rich histories of conflict into our home.

A good friend of mine often tells of how his family are talkers. With a clergyman, teacher, clinical psychologist, social worker and lawyer in the family, they do a lot of talking. He married a woman who came from a 'throw the plates across the table and scream' background. We need to understand these differences. One is neither better nor worse than another. Talking may seem optimum and when it never lets up, there is constant harking back to it, minutely exploring the hidden meanings – when the plate is thrown and it is over. We bring all these ways of expressing differences into the place we call work.

Now we come to see the multiple ways in which we can create an organisational conflict culture. Some organisations create cultures where feedback is a dangerous thing – or is perceived to be. Some organisations even go so far as to promote their challenging people rather than having to give them feedback or deal with behaviour.

And this is how we instantly also come to see the myths we can equally create around our conflict cultures. The feedback myth is a good example. Because we believe that in our culture we cannot give feedback, we never do – and what are the results?

Reach out and touch

This reminds me of an experience I had while coaching a senior executive. John was an interesting leader. As he was viewed by colleagues and staff as a bully, the Chief Executive of his organisation had asked me to work with him. And, before you ask, no-one had told him that he was seen as a bully, not even the CEO. We don't like to raise difficult things, do we?

Anyway, after unsuccessfully trying to see if I could get a colleague to take the job (me, I'm a coward from way back and working with bullies is not my favourite way of spending time), I met him for the first time. Everything seemed fine until I noticed someone hovering outside his office. The woman had one of those 'please help me to fall through the floor' looks about her. Eventually she entered the office and said with almost a stutter: "Um, so sorry but I was wondering, well sort of wondered, if you wanted me to attend this meeting with Charles as you asked yesterday, or should I wait?"

What happened next will stay etched in my brain forever. He held out his hand to her as he remained seated. She stretched her hand to meet his with a look of absolute confusion. He said: "Let me hold your hand in this decision-making, shall I?" I cannot remember what her response was as she scuttled out of the room like a puppy caught messing on the floor. His phone rang and he rushed out to deal with another emergency, saying he would see me as agreed the next week.

Well, like many others I have never inhaled and, for the next week, I kept thinking that I had imagined what had happened. As the time of his appointment drew nearer I felt more and more ill. How was I going to raise the bullying issue? It is in these moments that I feel like closing my business down and taking up carpentry (preferably on a warm island off the coast of Kenya).

When I finally raised this in our next meeting, John had no memory whatsoever of his actions. As I began to describe my reality in the meeting he became very concerned. We began to talk about how the more senior you become in an organisation the less likely people are to give you the gift of feedback. The strategy his organisation had employed was to avoid conflict by moving it on – promoting him out of one area to the next rather than challenging his behaviour.

Is John really a 'bully' or are all of the people around him in those various roles responsible with him for how he interacts with others? What is the culture they have created together?

Forming profitable cultures

The first step in creating a profitable culture is having the ability to understand the culture you are working in. How does it operate, how are things expressed, who are understood to be the key players, what are the assumptions you hold, what are the myths that have been created?

What are you noticing?

If cultures are formed by the conversations we have then a good starting point has to be with a renewed view of our communications.

We have to be brave to avoid the easy options of humour or management speak when something is at stake. And in our experience when we do take the courage to say something, it is rarely as bad as our worst fantasy.

I was facilitating a leadership programme in the UK. There had been wranglings in the group about racial differences. We wanted to create an environment where the group could name how they were feeling. Rather than force the conversation, we would let the issue emerge when the group was ready. Although it was a really tense debate, people trusted the group to hear what they had to say.

The amazing result was that people recognised different points of view, understood sensitivities that had not occurred to them and came out a stronger team. Many acknowledged that they had been too 'scared' to raise it, for concern about being labelled racist or tearing a good group apart or whatever.

Communication is never straightforward but it can be simple

Are we really 'seeing' communication for what it is? To many of us, communication seems straightforward, invisible. To others, it's actually part of the problem – something to be avoided.

How do we prompt people to think about what communication is for? Is it just to 'inform' (recognising that this is very important)? What else could it be achieving? To motivate? To create a shared vision of what could be possible in our Partnering? To innovate? To enable people to take the responsibility and to take the lead? To liberate people to create positive cultures – cultures that profit from the differences that exist?

We need to see communications as our most powerful conflict management tool. We don't need to focus on our communications 100% of time – only where it is critical, i.e. in our conflict. We do need to do this in a way that doesn't always see conflict as a negative. If we do not hold appreciation, good will and good intent towards people, our conflict with them can only go in one direction. A vicious circle develops. We create our own self-fulfilling prophecy about conflict. In many ways, it's seeing conflict in this totally negative way that stops us dealing with it wherever we see it.

The more we know about communication the less it seems we understand. This tells us one important thing – communication is chaos. If we send an e-mail to 10 people, they will understand it in 12 different ways. We can choose how we react to this. We can get angry that people are not listening or paying attention or are even wilfully misinterpreting our e-mail. Or we can get curious about what prevents them from listening or what exists in their lives that makes it important for them not to listen.

If we choose the latter, we learn to recognise the different realities that people hold. One person's bully is another's strong manager. A terrorist to one nation is a freedom fighter to the next. We learn that there are different realities about what a successful outcome means. For some, it's punishing someone, for others it's showing they're right. A lot of people want to win.

Any outcome can lead to more conflict. Someone is punished, someone is wrong, someone loses. Inevitably, people in conflict dehumanise each other – we lose any notion of 'good intent'. 'He's not a team player', 'She's always negative', 'Here comes trouble.' If I am in conflict with my manager, I see that any plan they have is about getting at me, rather than improving performance.

Conversations change cultures

Mostly, we can begin with the Partnering assumption that culture is created in conversation. The essence of how we create effective Partnering is in our conversations.

As I have mentioned earlier, we work with a cultural change strategy that has come to be known as StarFish conversations. We were using it with a major call centre in the UK that was facing a number of challenges – high staff turnover, young management team, exhausted post-takeover workforce, high customer complaints etc. StarFish enabled people to recognise the critical links between business and people issues in this highly charged and stressful call centre environment. StarFish put together a few of the techniques mentioned above that we use to work with conflict to get a vast number of people in conversation about what was working in business sections and what ideas could be put into practice to improve business performance.

Using the simple assumptions that cultures are formed in conversation and are guided by the questions we ask, the call centre achieved the following in six months: customer satisfaction increased by 30%, effective inter-departmental collaboration was boosted and customer complaints sent directly to the executive fell by 37%. 1,557 ideas were generated, 387 of which made cost savings of £726,500. Staff awareness of customer service increased, as levels of empowerment and morale soared. Adopting a Partnering ethos brings about transformational change within and between large organisations in record time with amazing results.

What's the question?

If conversations are an essential part of developing our ability to assume the position, then the questions that we ask which generate those conversations become an essential part of our Partnering skills.

When next you sit down with your partner – within your team or from another organisation – perhaps you could take a moment or two to chat around these questions:

What does the word conflict mean to you?

How would you describe the differences you notice between us?

What are the strategies you see us using to manage our differences?

How would you describe the culture that we have created together?

How will we cash in on our differences?

6
Questioning Power

Partnering needs the skill to ask affirmatively disruptive questions

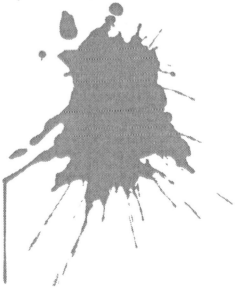

Are questions just questions?

How do you view questions?

What do you think about them?

How many do you ask in a day?

What do you want to achieve with each question?

What are you noticing about the impact your questions have, at different times, with different people?

Do you ever notice the impact that you have when you ask someone 'why'?

What are the questions you keep asking?

If I were to ask those around you what sort of questions you ask, would you be proud of their answer?

What questions, when asked of you, drive you nuts?

When did a question last take you in a completely different direction?

One of the exercises we often use when helping people to develop their questioning skills is a task that we set one week before we meet. We simply ask people to think about the most powerful question they have ever been asked – although not the 'will-you-marry-me, when-will-you-give-me-a-divorce?' sort. More the kinds of questions that stop you in your tracks, that you hear and then only think about weeks later, that help you to take a major leap in the way you think.

When the group meets up, the statements we hear from people are along the lines of: 'I couldn't find one single example', 'It was really difficult to remember', 'Did you mean a single question, because I thought of a conversation rather than a question?', 'Does it have to be a positive question?', 'I've never noticed questions before.'

People also notice all kinds of things about the examples they think of – the impact of timing, the relationship they had with the person then, the use of language, the state of their TICing model at the time. When people give examples, others in the group often struggle to see what was so powerful.

The purpose of the exercise is to get people to start noticing how we work with questions and the range of assumptions that cuddle up to each question that we ask. Where people really start getting interested and excited is when we ask them: "If I were privileged enough to come into your organisation in a year's time and ask the people who work with you about the most powerful question they have been asked, will they name you and your question?"

The power of a question

Many of us really struggle with accepting praise. We very quickly insist that it's nothing really, anyone could do whatever it is. Our friend Christine, the one who wondered what made me let life pass me by in Lagos, was chatting with my partner Sara. Everyone who meets Sara talks about how warm and gentle she is with people. How much of an interest she takes in the people she meets. Christine is a feisty lawyer type from Nigeria – a 'no nonsense, get-over-yourself' type of woman. She said to Sara that she aspired to be like Sara in her gentleness and warmth with people. True to her English form, Sara instantly said: "Oh no, Christine, it's not really like that." Christine was in like a shot: "Oh, so you are not being genuine?" Suddenly, for the first time, Sara could instantly see the impact we make when we refuse to accept positive feedback from people.

One thing Sara teaches people in her work day in and day out is the importance of focusing on what is working, of learning from strengths, of helping people to understand the detail of what is effective – and this was the first time that she'd had such a powerful insight in a way that has instantly changed how she responds to positive feedback. Since that conversation she has never tried to underplay, ignore or undermine feedback that is given to her.

What is the most powerful question you have ever been asked?

Stop.

Let your mind play with just a few of these questions for a moment. Have a go at becoming a question spotter for a while.

The power of affirmatively disruptive curiosity.

Effective Partnering can liberate people from feeling they have to know all the answers *and* challenge them to take responsibility for and pay attention to the questions they ask.

Our capacity to partner effectively is grounded in our ability to question in a way that urges us to be more curious, cashing in on the conflicts we have as a positive resource. If things are going to change effectively, the challenge is to disrupt things in a way that urges people to think differently and therefore begin to acquire a different attitude. We need to disrupt them so that the result is positive – an affirmative disruption.

If questions are a great way to make a huge impact – they disrupt people and direct them to think differently – then making a positive impact depends on more than just asking any questions. We need to ask *affirmative* questions that disrupt people in affirmative ways. Affirmatively disruptive questions can both create an immediate and long term shift *and* provide an opportunity for life long learning – you never know it all.

Graeme was facilitating a conversation with a group of people from one organisation who did not know each other. One said their IT support team was useless, never any good. Most of the group instantly jumped on the bandwagon. "Yeah, IT are a nightmare!"

When Graeme noticed that one person was silent, he decided to challenge the group. "Are you saying that IT are 'never' any help? I find it surprising that a business as smart as this one would resource a team that provides no value. What are some of the services and experiences that you have had where they have done a good job?"

After a short pause a few different responses began trickling out, soon turning into a flood. "Well, actually, I had a problem last week and I phoned the help desk and they helped me sort it in 10 mins." And, "I did get my machine replaced within 48 hours after I dropped it." Not to mention, "My anti-virus software gets updated automatically, so I don't even know it's happening."

Graeme followed this feedback by saying how interesting it was that we don't remember these things very clearly. He wondered out loud what it was like being in the IT team, doing your best everyday and only hearing one story back. He then asked the silent person where he worked and received the reply, "In the IT support team." Graeme asked him what it was like. "It can be a bit dispiriting." Graeme asked him what he thought of this conversation. "It's great to hear that people do recognise we do our best."

At this point, of course, everyone chorused that IT did a good job. The man from the IT support team had been silenced by the earlier conversation. Graeme used the situation as an opportunity to get people in the room to question themselves about the assumptions they held in an affirmative way that countered the cynicism.

Through the kind of questions he asked, he was directing people to stop, think and see that it was possible to pay attention and help IT to do a great job. This did not deny that IT had some challenges. Graeme gave some examples of how people's conversations with IT could be different next time. "When I had a problem last week you were really helpful and sorted it over the phone." Or, "Because you responded instantly, I didn't miss any of my targets." And, "This time it is taking rather longer and you are now saying we can't sort it until tomorrow. How could we work like last time to get it sorted today, so we can both go home?"

The art of questioning

We cannot hope to develop the art of questioning if we do not pay attention to developing and refining it on a daily basis. For me, it is an endless pursuit. I'm eternally fascinated by what prompts me to ask certain questions at certain times of myself or others. What makes me respond to questions in one way on one day and then completely differently on another day?

How do I hope to get ahead when, with all good intent, I can never be certain of how my question will be heard?

A good starting point is by seeing that questioning is indeed an art – interpreted differently by different people, having the capacity to shift and move people or leave them where they are. Each one of us will develop our own particular style of questioning.

If you don't believe me, just take a moment next time you're in the office to listen in to someone's telephone conversation. What's their style? Do they preface the conversation with questions asking after the other's health, children, night out, recent holiday? Or do they dive straight into the reason for the call? If so, what questions are they asking to get the knowledge they need? Does the call seem to be going well? If not, what questions are being asked to change the direction of the conversation?

As soon as we understand that it is an art we will recognise that we have no control over how our questions are heard. And that is a good leap forward. It is obvious that, when acquiring the attitude, we need to hold onto our curiosity and start really noticing the impact of the questions we ask and the direction in which we're taking people.

We do not control thinking with questions, we just create opportunities for people to consider new directions. Therefore, we need to listen to the answers and go with the flow, see where they take us and maintain our curiosity.

In this, we need to pay careful attention to the chaos – how we intend our question to be heard may not be the way it is heard.

CAN OF WORDS – POLITICAL CORRECTNESS

It's difficult to find people who support political correctness. It's an easy target. Yet, think again. Partnering talks about paying attention to how we speak and how we hear others. Surely, we can't dismiss political correctness so easily? The term 'political correctness' was apparently coined in the 1920s yet championed in the 1990s by journalists to describe the language used by people who care about the sensitivities of disadvantaged people. The media has largely ensured that, although the *intention* behind political correctness is a positive attempt to re-humanise, many people now associate the *practice* with the avoidance of the 'truth'. As a result, for these people, actively avoiding naming in a judgemental way leaves too much unsaid. And people who care about language and meaning are silenced. When we condemn what we see as 'political correctness', however, are we merely criticising the unsatisfactory nature of the language, the *practice*, saying 'What use are words if we cannot use them?' If so, I wonder why the English love euphemism so much. Or, are we condemning the intention behind it, asking to return to a time when it was acceptable to de-humanise people in contexts we have not bothered to understand? If so, what does that say about our sense of justice or humanity? Partnering techniques can help us keep the *intention* and the *practice* together and find different forms of language to challenge other people's assumptions about what a person is or could be. We learn to listen for the meaning, so that the feeling and the intent will help us to hear and respond most appropriately and effectively.

Questioning is a gentle art

We were working with a team of people in a civil service department. We were told that people were feeling a bit despondent due to recent changes in the department. Would we do some work with them to help them to see things differently and learn about working more effectively with their differences?

To kick the day off, we came up with an excellent new exercise. As a way of getting people warmed up and into the magical world of questioning, we put the group into three teams. Each team was given a ball of paper. The game was simple. Throw the paper to someone else, let them open it and read out one of the questions written on it. Then we asked the group to instantly respond to the question. A way of getting people to notice the impact of questions.

With any game of this nature we decide to start with a simple question, just to help people understand the rules. Now, we see ourselves as pretty hot at this questioning stuff, so we crafted a simple, positive, fun, light-hearted question to get them going: "How will your social life be different when you get your driver's licence?"

One person responded immediately with: "Do you think I have a drinking problem?" Another said: "So, you think I haven't got any friends now?"

As each of the three groups had a similar response, we wondered what on earth was going on. Clearly, we had not gauged the level of cynicism and mistrust in the organisation, to the extent that virtually everyone regarded any question put to them with fear and suspicion. We had asked those questions in open faith, but that is not how they were heard.

Only later did we find out that this was an organisation where people felt shafted by internal change that had gone pear-shaped. The entire organisation had been restructured; everyone had to re-apply for their jobs. Those that did not have one were told first, then, in sympathy with their colleagues, those that had jobs refused to take them. Ultimately, the leader was moved to another organisation and everyone was re-hired.

Unsurprising then, that people did not trust the intentions of some outsiders! We'd been trying to motivate people with affirmative intervention questions, when we'd have done better to stick with questions of the most basic kind that built trust.

Hindsight is easy – we went in on the good Partnering assumption of holding good will and intent towards people, and that's not how we were received. But the main point still stands – that, for many people, sharing opinions, ideas and possibilities has to be built on foundations of trust.

Clearly, there is no such thing as a neutral question to all hearers. It follows that, if we've made the effort to understand the significant influences of the hearer, how can we then question to understand how we have been heard?

What is the purpose of your question?

No sooner do I need to remind myself each time it happens – that I have no control over how someone will hear a question – than I am jolted right back to thinking about what my purpose is.

What is the purpose of the question? We need to be clear about that. We want to know where it is taking us.

We sometimes seem to assume that we only ask questions for information. What other purposes do we have for questions? To attack someone's idea, make a point, get someone to ask us a question? "Where did you go on holiday?" To motivate, inspire, cover our back, attract. "Do you come here often?" "What does your partner do? Oh, you haven't got one?"

Questioning is a tool that can have a huge impact and it's readily available to everyone.

How many opportunities are you missing out on – times when, with a simple question, you could shift an entire group, stop people from travelling down a road to nowhere, make people smile at themselves?

I came across one organisation that was investing thousands of pounds in demotivating and demoralising its employees and its customers. They told me that their key priorities were to create an empowering culture and to improve customer service – and yet they could not see that what they were doing was creating the exact opposite effect.

Here is how it worked. Every six months, each employee was instructed to put aside half an hour to complete a questionnaire. I seem to remember that they called it a staff opinion survey. The questionnaire focused their attention on the times they felt disempowered, the incompetence of management, the lack of career progression. As people walked away from their work stations, having completed the compulsory questionnaire, they reminded themselves of their New Year's resolution to find another job, sell up and travel around the world, get another life, any life that wasn't this. Then they began to realise it was the fault of management, the organisation, the colleague next to them who never lifts a finger.

And out they go to meet with customers because it is important to get their feedback. They walk into the customer's factory. Things are humming, business is brisk, the customer is chattering away about something that happened the previous week that this supplier had gone all out to resolve and they had now secured a new contract. As the two people sit down and have a coffee, our weary worker gets on with his job. "Yeah, great! And tell me where do we disappoint you? What do we need to change? How many times have we let you down over the last few months? What do other suppliers give you that we can't?" And they leave the meeting connected by their collective misery! The customer realising what a fool she had been, decides its time to find a new supplier!

If we focus on what we're not doing very well – '13% of our customers do not think we give great customer service' – there is a strong likelihood that we'll change processes and systems that undermine the way from which 87% of our customers benefit.

If the questions we ask determine the direction we take – both for individuals and organisations – where are you taking people every day?

Would it be better to focus on what we do well together, in order to tackle what we don't?

Acquire your Partnering attitude

What's your attitude?

The way we behave stems from the kind of questions we ask in the first place. So, perhaps a useful starting point is for us to reflect on the attitudes we adopt when questioning.

Most of us take up different attitudes at different times. Some of us tend towards a particular perspective or attitude most of the time.

Sometimes, I find myself in conversations with people about the difference between truth and spin, between asking about the facts and creating unrealistic fantasies. What is it that makes us think questions that discover what is *not working*, that focus on *judging situations*, that extract a *hidden* truth, are seen as objective questions? Are we talking about the aspiration of many journalists to find that kind of truth, because we all know that bad news sells?!

And yet, when we get into questions that focus our attention on what is working, that find out *different ways* of *viewing things*, that seek to *illuminate meaning*, suddenly this is spin and we are accused of influencing the answers by the questions we ask.

We have a choice to take either direction. Neither is a particular truth – it is simply the focus and direction we have decided to take. Oh, and by the way, one of my assumptions is that good news sells – we just need the opportunity to buy it!

Are we judge, jury and executioner?

We are all quick to judge – others, decisions, situations, circumstances, and, probably most frequently, ourselves. It clearly has its uses – it's all part of the human selective ability that makes us discriminating and successful inhabitants of this planet. Most of the time we don't even know we're doing it. Adopting a critical eye has become second nature: seeing without noticing.

In the time that it takes to convert what we've seen but not noticed into verbal communication, something happens. Or, in most cases, fails to happen. We do not use that gap to stand back, assess and deliberate as well as we might. When we engage our minds then our mouths, we can pay very little attention to the way our words might be received and are received.

Communication is disruptive. It's meant to be. We communicate to change one state of being into another. What more disruptive form of communication is there than to ask somebody a question? You tend to sit up and take notice. Just as you have a range of options for the way you answer, so the person who put the question in the first place had a range of reasons for asking. Just because we do it every day most of the time, we should not assume that communication is straightforward.

Within organisations people ask many questions of each other all the time. Next time you ask somebody a question, watch how it affects them, mentally and physically. People literally go in the direction that we question them. The way people react to our questions and the way we respond to theirs often determines the nature of our whole relationship.

Could we be creator, contributor and enabler?

In moments when we are not fleeing a herd of rampaging elephants or not about to make a parachute jump for charity, we can switch our focus from 'judge' to 'create'. That is, most of the time, whenever we want, if we learn how to do it.

Instead of judge, jury and executioner, we can be creator, contributor and enabler in any conversation. As long as we're clear on the purpose of our question, of every question.

If we take time to notice how people react to questions, we can learn to ask questions that not only give us the answers we are seeking, they give life to people and liberate them to act differently.

In this way, before we open our mouths we begin to listen to our own internal questioner. Then, even in the most conflict-ridden situation, the first and most powerful question becomes the one that we ask ourselves:

How can I ask my question in a way that feeds the relationship? That gives life?

We are faced with our internal voice many times, every day. We switch on the TV news. A man is arrested after being on the run for three weeks. His crime? Beating up an old-age pensioner to steal £27. We see and hear this. We must react. If, however, we are training ourselves to assume the position and take on board some useful Partnering assumptions, our thinking might quickly jump from asking the question, 'How can we punish him?' (a judgement on a past we cannot change) to 'How can we awaken his conscience?' (the possibility of a future we can influence). We have the choice to take either position. Which is best for society? It's not rocket science. Or maybe it is as a medical scientist once told me that rocket science is easy!

Who asks the questions? Who knows the answers?

If questions are all-powerful, who asks the questions and who knows the answers? Often, as leaders, our instinct is to feel we need to give the answer and quickly.

What if we began to see that it was more important to let any question prompt us to think? To create a gap between the question put to us and the response we give?

Thinking about people's assumptions in relation to our own enables us to grasp the meaning of the chaos of communication. This is what encourages us to get more curious and see how important it is for all of us to be asking questions.

The truly great thing about asking affirmatively disruptive questions in a Partnering relationship is that it allows us to get beyond our own sense of what winning is. As we described back in Chapter 2, rather than 'Win-Win', we can achieve what we call a 'Both-Gain' outcome. It's a bit different from 'Win-Win'. We're asking questions that enable us to do great work – and that can be challenging.

Questions for Partnering success

While it's great fun and highly instructive to focus on noticing the questions you hear all around you, then thinking about their meaning and purpose, the ultimate point of the exercise is to set about asking useful and powerful questions yourself. What kinds of question are there? Where do you start? And how?

Two kinds of Partnering questions

When I introduce people to the power of questions in Partnering situations, I group them into two kinds:

questions for understanding

questions for intervention

When we want to know something, it's quite common to leap straight into questions for understanding. We are impatient and want to get to the point. In situations of conflict and difference, however, before we leap to ask questions of others it is useful to pay attention to the voices in our own heads.

We need to notice our internal voice – what are the questions we ask ourselves? As with any form of questioning, it's where we begin that sets the tone. Is my starting point that you are not trustworthy and so I look for evidence that supports this? It's bound to arrive sooner or later. Or, is my starting point one of good intent, shown by my willingness to believe you're doing everything for the best of reasons?

Moving beyond starting points, we need to keep a constant eye on where our internal voice is taking us. As soon as something happens that begins to create a question in our minds as to someone's motive or intention, we need to learn to be alert to these shifts in attitude and immediately have a conversation to address it. In the context of Partnering, we need to question our internal questioner, check out our assumptions and return to a position of trust as soon as possible.

How can my internal questioner help me to see multiple realities, understand significant influences and promote Partnering relationships?

The second thing we need to do about our own assumptions is to question them out loud, explicitly, in conversation. And it takes courage to ask these questions. At the end of a meeting, I ask: "What is your understanding of what I am trying to achieve?" I'm being brave, as you have the opportunity to cut me down: "You are playing out your agenda again". If you don't cut me down, we increase our capacity to give and receive feedback.

The ways in which you interpreted, understood, concluded and analysed the actions, e-mails, correspondence, inaction, words, comments and silences – the wonderful, crazy and very sound logic that you came to that then led to thinking about questioning your trust in the person or organisation. If you are brave enough to take this attitude, you will learn a lot about how you think, help the other person to understand the links you make and build another foundation in the moving world of trust.

Questions for understanding

Why is this like this? Why did you do that? Why are we even doing this? The next time somebody asks you a question beginning with 'Why', stop for a second and gauge how you feel. Are you experiencing a slight rise in body temperature? Is your skin pricking? Are you about to respond in a defensive or even aggressive manner? Are you like the mother in the store who's had one too many 'Whys' inviting her three year old to go and ask God herself? We probably ask more questions for understanding than any other kind. We are curious animals, we simply want to know. So we ask questions to deepen and broaden our understanding. However, if we begin from the assumption that our need to know overrides someone else's desire to inform us in a way that makes sense to them, we're likely to get off on the wrong foot. Effective Partnering needs us to learn to question in a way that enables people to hold their opinions lightly.

The person who asked you that 'Why' question is in 'judge' mode. You may not be clear on the reason they asked you that particular question, yet how are you feeling? You may even have been expecting the 'Why' question, yet you are still feeling put on the spot. Who likes to be judged? More than likely, the person who asked the question does not understand the full context you're in. Which is, of course, partly why they asked (although you will never know exactly how much, unless you ask them!).

How funny it is that we often respond to a 'Why' question with one in return. Why are you asking me? Why versus why. Take that back. Touché! When we do this, what we're saying is, 'Re-phrase your meaning!' We're asking the aggressor (for that is how we perceive them) to put into context the particular meaning behind the simple question. As we're individual beings with complex lives, this meaning could be anything: 'I haven't got time to mess about', 'I've got a train to catch/budget to meet', 'I hate meetings', 'My wife's just asked me for a divorce', 'Chelsea didn't win last night', 'They used to do this to me in my last company', 'I'm a winner with a reputation to keep up.'

Why not 'why' questions? There are two main benefits: we move away from conversations with 'because' answers *and* we have a greater capacity to notice our questions and their impact. Questions for understanding help us to pay attention to the different meanings people give to words and events. They also help us to make connections to our TICing models – the way we are feeling about significant influences on our lives at any given time.

Questions for intervention

When we ask questions for intervention, we are actively trying to enable a change of direction in the conversation. They're very important to Partnering relationships, as they help us think (and therefore act) differently. Some conversations are less than useful. For Partnering to flourish, we need tools that enable us to move on to other possibilities. As such, questions for intervention are more complex than questions for understanding or trust-building.

Getting people to think differently means urging them to see possibilities rather than problems. So, Partnering encourages us to learn the difference between embedding positive and negative suggestions.

This is where people usually ask the purpose of 'leading questions'. We are familiar with these and they feel uncomfortable. This is because they are based on your answers that you have already decided on and that you are leading us towards. We feel manipulated to agree with you. A friend of mine recently told me of a referendum question he was considering not

Cash in on Conflict

answering. In disagreement with the long-term plans of the District Council on new house building in its part of town, a local residents' association had forced a referendum which asked all town residents the following question: 'As our town has already fulfilled its quota for house building, should any land that is undeveloped be allocated for housing?'

Although the question indicates that the whole situation is clearly complex, the main thing we take from it is that it is a leading question. The whole point of a leading question is that it ignores anybody else's point of view – in this case, the District Council and those people who elected it, and people in other parts of the town.

My friend says he has sympathy with the views of the residents' association, but that the District Council has been at pains to communicate a plan that will safeguard that part of town from developers for the next decade, whereas failing to lay out a plan would open up the land to legal challenges from developers.

Is it typical of people who are not listening to want to get others to agree with their own point of view at any cost? And to ratify that in the form of a leading question? What do you think? Whatever, my friend was considering not answering what he saw as a leading question. While this was his democratic prerogative, it turned out that 84% of his fellow potential voters also chose not to exercise their right to vote. Of the 16% who did vote, 95% inevitably voted No. So, on a contentious issue, only around 15% of the electorate gave a definitive answer. My friend assumed that, like him, many people just did not see the point in answering a leading question that was attempting to control their way of thinking...
even if they agreed with its sentiment!

If we're asking questions for intervention in a Partnering relationship we're not trying to lead people towards the answer we want. Instead, we're creating possibilities by offering different ways to think about something.

We can make our questions a gift to people

When we ask questions, we usually want answers right then and there. Quite a lot of the time, however, if we were to just step back and consider the value of our Partnering relationship, we would phrase our question as a gift. 'Here is something in which I would value your input. Can we discuss your thoughts tomorrow?' It can be useful to give people time to think about our question before we need an answer.

Having been in his job for five or six years, Graeme's friend was restless and looking for a new challenge. Over recent months he had been grappling with what he wanted to do next with his life and where he wanted to work. Finally, he found an advert for a job that he was really excited about. He prepared thoroughly and was granted an interview. Knowing that he was to hear whether he had been successful, Graeme phoned him up. He knew from the dull tone of his friend's voice that all was not well.

When Graeme asked his friend for his news he replied that he had failed to get the job, that he was disillusioned with the search for a different career and that he had decided to stay where he was. Even though he was unhappy with the current situation, there was no point carrying on as he would never succeed.

Graeme could hear the pain in his voice and sympathised with him. He wanted to help his friend out but did not know what to tell him. And then he thought about his own work at Questions of Difference and the power of questions – the idea that questions can give life and that people go in the direction that we question.

So Graeme began asking his friend a few carefully considered questions. "They invited you to an interview, so they must have seen something in you that they found interesting. What feedback did they give you about your strengths in relation to this kind of work?"

His friend recalled that they did give him some good feedback. "They said that I have all the relevant experience and a good approach – it was simply that one of the other candidates had worked in the industry for longer, so they offered the job to her rather than me." Graeme probed a little deeper. "You haven't previously been able to put your finger on the type of job that you are really after. I know that you were very keen on this particular job. Having done all that preparation and having met the people at that organisation, I expect you have a much clearer idea of what you want to be doing. What have you learnt from this experience about the type of job you would like?"

Graeme's friend answered by affirming that, yes, researching this company had shown him it was possible to find a job where he could combine the two areas he was really interested in – working both on the development of policy and getting out of the office and meeting real people. "That's what I need to be doing!"

Graeme then asked: "Where did you find the advert for this job?" The answer was very positive. "That's interesting. For the first time I started searching for job adverts on the internet – you can find loads of recruitment sites there... OK, I've got to go. I need to get on with updating my CV to focus more specifically on the type of job that I want. After that, there are several recruitment sites I haven't looked at yet. I should be able to get several applications out before Monday, and could have a couple of interviews lined up in a week or two."

As Graeme put the phone down he wondered if his friend had consciously tuned in to his intention of helping him move on positively. Did that matter? The questions he asked had sought out what had worked and sparked his friend's imagination for what could now be possible. Their conversation demonstrated that people really do go in the direction that we question them. So, what impact do we want to have on those around us and what life-giving questions will we ask?

Last but not least, when we get used to asking our partners great affirmatively disruptive questions, it's worth noting that people are taking longer to respond than they used to. In which case, one of the best things we can do is sit in silence.

A great question prompts people to think, so let them.

7

Cash In

... and get on with
Partnering!

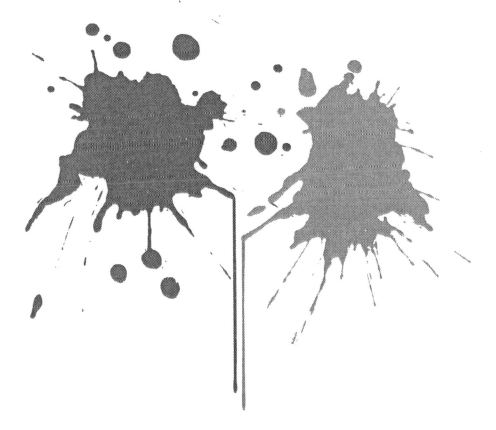

Turning from thoughts to action

You will be clear by now that a lot of what it takes to cash in on conflict sits in your head. How you think about things, how you notice things and the assumptions you throw into the mix.

In challenging ourselves to exploit conflict and leap into the world of questions, we have focused much of our discussion on our capacity to think ourselves into a Partnering DNA.

It's a most useful skill when we can take an idea or a different way of thinking and instantly apply it to what is in front of us. Better still, apply it in a way that fits with who we are, integrating it into just the way things are done, so that we are more likely to create the differences we want.

Our final chapter aims to do just that. We are going to look at a range of situations and explore some easy-to-apply and common sense approaches that we hope will help you and your partners to achieve your outcomes.

The situations we will explore include:

Partnering with individuals at work – is there someone driving you nuts? What could be different?

Partnering within teams – you just know you are not greater than the sum of the parts – what's going on?

Partnering between teams – being stuck in your silos and not being able to lift your head to see what else is going on in your organisation, the big talked-about issue that never gets resolved!

Partnering between organisations – by choice or force, you have to create a different way of working with them if you want to retain or establish a competitive advantage.

Getting it right from the start – do we develop strategies for setting up a Partnering relationship with a strong foundation, or do we carry on jumping in with our eyes closed and fingers crossed that this time it will work out?

The end of the chapter finds us wandering in the world of curiosity again with questions that focus on 'what could be different?'.

Getting on with Partnering

Partnering with individuals

Our daily interactions with the range of individuals we work with have a significant impact on our days. Could be that there are some people we really rely on, others we barely notice are even there and others whom our patient families know more about than they want to.

Those you love

You may think it strange to focus on the people you get on really well with. One of the most important reasons to do this is to learn from what is working, so that you can apply this to the other working relationships that you have and develop.

Try taking an hour or so over coffee with one of the people you work really well with, someone that you would name if I were to ask you to give me an example of when you partner really well with someone at work. During your conversation you might want to begin with a general chat about Partnering. Have they read the book? What are their thoughts and insights?

Would they describe the way you work together as Partnering?

What are you noticing about how you work together – how you communicate, disagree about things, come up with ideas together, complement and compliment each other? What are the assumptions you both hold when working together, when receiving a piece of work from each other? Which of the Partnering assumptions we have suggested would be useful to discuss and explore? Have you been in conflict? How do you really exploit the differences between you?

Finally, you might find it interesting to ask them things about how they think or work that they know you are not aware of – and how you could strengthen your mutual ability to exploit the differences between each other.

Much like a savings account, it may be useful to then take a few moments to make a mental note of the things you discussed and deposit them for future use. These will be useful for you either in times of stress with this individual or, more importantly, when you begin to explore how you could partner with those you ignore and those you hate!

Those you ignore

You may well need to start by paying attention to those you ignore to even discover who they might be. Who are these people? And what on earth is prompting you to ignore them? Do you assume they have nothing to offer you? That they would not be interested in engaging with you, learning from you? What is it about how they are, the work they do, or what you assume that helps them to be invisible to you? What does this help you to notice about how you may or may not be exploiting the resources around you?

I focus on this area for one key reason – every single time I work with an organisation I discover people that the organisation does not know it has. In one organisation the tea lady turned out to be a retired head teacher, taking a different job after decades of great service to education, for her own good reasons. She was listening in to the training programme we had and helped some of the younger participants in the break with the concepts they were grappling with. When we invited her to open the annual conference in front of 300 people, the senior management team thought she was someone who worked for QoD – she had only served them tea every week for two years! Leaders are everywhere when you look for them.

If you have a lead role in your organisation you may want to take this a step further. How many people in your organisation actually sit in the 'ignored' world?

How many people on your payroll are unable to partner with the organisation in a way they know is making a difference?

Does your management team have the skills and capacity to really exploit all the differences people bring for maximum effect?

Those you hate

Our starting point here is that you have got to want to cash in on conflict. When we run a programme on managing difficult people it is amazing how many people arrive with the person they want to manage clearly in mind – and it is never themselves!

One strategy could be to have a conversation – ask them what effective working together for the two of you would mean for them. Try asking about some of the assumptions they hold and help them to see what you hold. Ask them who they currently partner effectively with – what can you both learn from that and the chat you had with the person you work well with? And, of course, it may be helpful to review Chapter 5 before asking them these questions. A question that could be heard as 'So, tell me about just one other person that you actually Partner with,' may not be expressed in so many words and could be heard in as many words.

If talking to them seems too radical perhaps you could start by noticing something different – about how other people might be working with them, getting the best from the way they partner together. Maybe you could choose one of the assumptions we discussed in Chapter 4, hold it whenever you are working with this person and see what happens. Perhaps you could pay some attention to the questions you exchange between you.

What is the purpose of your questions? Are they questions to give life or to deflate? Questions to encourage or questions that provoke? Questions that affirm or questions that punish?

What is your starting position or what position do you end up in? What is the impact of those questions, what are the assumptions you are making about their purpose in asking you those things, how could the language you are both using be contributing to the issues?

As these things begin to shift the way you are thinking and interacting with them, it may create enough space in your head for you to realise how much of your time, energy, and passion it is taking and how much patience is required on the part of others to maintain the status quo with this individual. This may well compel you to take action and sort it out. I have seen the absolute relief felt by individuals who have held animosities between themselves for months or years, when issues are finally resolved.

I know that you might be tempted to say that for the particular individual you are uniquely dealing with, there is no hope, you have no choice, it cannot be different, you have tried and nothing works. Well, perhaps – and I wonder? Do you think they would say the same about you? Are you the one that is beyond reasonableness? I would not have thought so.

Partnering within teams

What's the point?

What is the purpose and what are the outcomes? How many teams in your organisation could you instantly identify where every single team member is clear on the outcomes the team is trying to achieve and what its purpose is? My guess is that, if you took the time to check this out, over 90% of teams would have different understandings of this within their team.
It is critical to focus on purpose and outcomes. Unless we are clear on this, it becomes impossible to decide what good Partnering within the team will mean.

I suspect that one of the reasons most of us groan when our manager or leader decides to take us all away for a day to discuss our vision and mission, our focus for the year or whatever grand objective we have, is that our typical experience of these dreaded 'away days' is varying levels of nausea – we get back to the office no clearer on what difference it makes to the day job.

I am not knocking visions and missions. However, in some organisations they are designed by the top team in a top hotel with top editors and designers turning it into something the rest of us are tasked with memorising. Little wonder that we cannot remember.

If you are prepared for the challenge, take some time with your team and really try to get to the bottom of what outcomes you are really trying to achieve and how they inform the purpose of the team. Less of the grand words and more about what they actually need to do to get the job done. How does what this team do move the organisation closer to the outcomes it wants to achieve? And finally, what does each individual in the team understand by the term Partnering?

Meeting madness

One of the great human means of communicating, especially within organisations, is to meet. With this desire to communicate effectively with everyone in the team through meeting together comes another imperative – meetings about meetings. Suddenly, we find we have too many meetings, too many people being invited to attend, wasting time. There is no preparation as 'I have just come from another meeting', people start not attending as they have better things to do. Thankfully, for some of you, the advent of blueberries, raspberries and gooseberries means that you can now clear all your emails while sitting in the meeting.

Frustrated, we start to find alternative strategies – meetings with no seats ('That will shut them up'); 10-minute meetings that never run over no matter what; new meeting rules up there in meetings rooms for everyone to follow. Apart from developing varicose veins from standing so much, we are no further forwards in resolving the meeting dilemma.

Some things that may help you to stop the meeting madness in your organisation could be...

Take some time with each person in the team, on their own, to understand what they have noticed about meetings, the role they play in them, the role others play, the outcomes that are produced, the dynamics that go on, the issues that keep coming up. Through this, come to identify with them the assumptions they hold.

As a team, discuss the conversations you have all had. What are you noticing about this team and the meetings it has? If there was just one thing that the team could change that you think would have the biggest impact – do it! What would it take for everyone to value themselves and the team enough to actually prepare for each meeting – being clear on the purpose, outcomes and background.

If this seems like hard work – stop all meetings for two weeks and see what happens. What have you gained as a result, what is actually just working, and what have you missed? What is this telling you about your meetings?

Unlocking excellence

Are you by any chance the strategic team? The senior leadership team? The Board of Directors, Trustees? You all know that your job is to focus on strategy. How many times do you think to yourself, 'This is just detail, day-to-day stuff – what are we taking time on this for?'

Take a moment of honesty with yourself – do you know what strategic meetings for this team would actually look like? What would you be talking about, focusing on? What are the strengths, experiences, areas of expertise that every other member around the Board would bring to that particular topic? My guess is that a lot of us would not really know the depth of what others on the team are bringing.

Take yourselves out of the normal conversations and give the time to really discuss what it would mean to operate as a strategic team. A simple solution, if you are brave enough – from tomorrow, take 40% of what you do out of your diary and either dump it or delegate it. Now you have the time to unlock the excellence that sits within the team.

CAN OF WORDS – STRATEGIC

Have you ever even discussed what being 'strategic' means? My hypothesis is that most people who sit on so-called strategic teams have been promoted onto them, working their way up from an operational or technical background. In a world where the more senior you get the less you tend to ask questions for clarity, the more people remain silent about what they don't know. They come into these teams and are amazed at the topics of debate and how they are run. We don't even need to be on the team to realise this. Just give one member of the organisation a chance to attend one of these meetings as an observer and all their fantasies about the depth and complexity of these debates are dashed.

Partnering between teams

I'll show you mine if you show me yours

One of the biggest obstacles to effective working between teams is the phenomenal number of assumptions and 'bad will' intentions that teams often hold about each other. Of course, for them the assumptions are built on hard and fast evidence gathered over a long period of time. Add this to the systems and procedures within organisations that often enforce a silo approach and the aspiration to have good cross-functional and divisional working remains just that – aspirational.

As we see, when we are struggling within one team to be really clear on our purpose and outcome, managing our own meetings in curious ways and unable to unlock the potential within the team, then ensuring that we are effective when Partnering with another team adds to the complexity of the challenge.

A good start would be to invite an open conversation around the assumptions you hold about each other. It may surprise you a little that we suggest you begin by simply discussing the notion of what an assumption is. You may remember the example we used of the team whose members struggled with the notion of an assumption until they were given a chance to put the facts up. And, of course, people then realised that most if not all of the 'facts' were indeed assumptions.

You may find it useful to explore the assumptions people hold using themes or topics to focus the conversation. These could be assumptions about leadership, decision-making, priorities, communication, vested interest, hidden agendas and collaboration.

In Chapter 4, we presented seven assumptions from our experience. If you take some time with the team to think about the notion of assumptions and understand what some of the current assumptions are, you could agree on two or three assumptions that you will all commit to holding for a period of time and then see what is happening.

This conversation may lead you to realise just how much you do or don't understand about each other's worlds. Helping other teams to understand the issues you are grappling with, the pressures that you are under and the targets the organisation is driving you towards, could help the other teams to get a sense of what it is to be in your shoes. And, as someone once said, if you travel a mile in someone else's shoes then at a minimum you will be a mile away from them and have their shoes.

Get your MITS off!

It could be that there is a conflict or incident that has occurred that now makes it challenging for the teams to work effectively together. You have seen in Chapter 5 what this sort of thing is really costing you.

In Chapter 5 we focused on the world of conflict and introduced the notion of understanding where the differences lie. You will remember the four areas of focus: *Me* – what's my bad hair day issue? *Individuals* – what lies between two individuals? *Team* – how do the teams contribute? *System* – how do established systems contribute?

There is no more valuable tool than the MITS when dealing with the relationships between two teams or departments or divisions within one organisation. When getting the MITS off it may be useful to reflect on this question:

Who stands to lose or gain by this issue or conflict being resolved?

This might help you to get to the core of the issue.

Finally, it may be that what is required is the skills of an external facilitator. Someone from outside your team or even outside your business. Sometimes it is really useful to have someone who has no vested interest in the issues, who can come in with genuine curiosity, to help the different groups notice what is happening and help you to understand the assumptions people are holding. And make sure that they work in a way that helps people to move on with skills that ensure this sort of dynamic does not develop again.

Partnering between organisations

What do you mean?

As we chatted about in Chapter 2, the great thing about Partnering is that there is no model. Every interaction between two organisations can be defined and explained in myriad ways. Some would say that they have a strictly customer–supplier relationship. The customer is king and always right. Are they? Really? If I am the customer and I am not right, I want my suppliers to tell me. And yet, when we see the people within these organisations interact we notice a number of things. In joint meetings you can sometimes not tell which person comes from which organisation – the issue they are discussing seems to be owned by everyone.

Other organisations trumpet their commitment to building mutual relationships with their partner organisations and then revert to claiming the throne of customer when decisions are taken in the interests of their organisation alone.

We have recently been working with a multi-billion-pound organisation. The kind of organisation that talks about their own need to shift their culture. They see themselves as arrogant with their customers, let alone suppliers. They are so big, with so much power, that their sense of themselves is they can do most anything they choose. And yet, coming from QoD, a small consultancy organisation, we were curious about what it would be like to consult to them – one of their thousands of suppliers. Lambs to the slaughter?! We have never been better treated. The executive team often behaves more as though we are the customers, the finance department has a 100% commitment to never paying small suppliers late, the legal department advised us on how best to protect our intellectual property – and yet they seem to think they do not partner well.

We promised common sense in this chapter. If your organisation is committed to developing effective and profitable relationships with other organisations, then the simple starting point is to have a conversation with them to understand the following:

For your organisation and theirs, at this time, given your objectives and theirs, your future vision and theirs, what would an effective Partnering relationship look like? How would the executives be interacting with each other, what tweaks to your respective systems could you make, how could working in this way help each of you to change elements of your existing cultures that are holding you back?

Sacred COWS

Exploring the sacred cows between your organisations could prove to be a really useful strategy for you: Culture, Ownership, Wedding and Systems.

How much of your own culture do you understand and are able to put into words that make sense for others?

What is your organisation's conflict culture? What are the range of 'that's the way things are done around here' assumptions that you don't even realise you are holding? What do people tell you about the culture when they first join your organisation? Do you even bother to ask them or, in your eagerness to integrate them into your way of doing things, do you lose this vital intelligence?

Given the degree to which we sometimes do not understand our own organisational cultures, it is little wonder that we may have even less of an idea about the culture of our partners' organisations. Start noticing and naming what you both see – I guarantee that a number of the things they have done in the past, decisions they have taken, will suddenly become a lot clearer to you.

The next area to explore is questions of ownership between organisations who partner. Who owns what? By this, I do not mean buildings and equipment. I mean who owns what rights. The right to take the decision, the right to own the concept, the right to dismiss a priority, the right not to respond, the right to walk away, the right to issue ultimatums.

Who owns the power? And just as important, who owns the risk? Who stands to lose more, and who is perceived to lose more?

These are by no means easy conversations to have. What I would like to argue for, however, is that far less time and energy will be spent on these conversations than on those we currently have within our own organisations, hypothesising about our partners' hidden agendas.

What were your dreams, fantasies and hopes for the future when you tied the knot? How much did you invest in the wedding and what sort of marriage do you now have?

Is it the one you dreamed of when you were a little girl? White veils and rugged handsome chivalry? Or is it sullen silence? Drunken violence and dreams of what might have been? You will remember from Chapter 1 the 20-year conflict between two organisations that was resolved in one day by inviting people to think about a divorce. We use the analogy of weddings and divorce to illustrate the degree to which individual beliefs, assumptions and emotional connection to what it means to partner is brought into what we assume to be strictly business.

Systems can be very helpful to people and they can drive us nuts. Any one of us who could relate to the mother in the video store attempting and failing to take out a DVD due to the system, will see the power that we in organisations give to systems. If you are really going to partner with an organisation then you need to be prepared to take a long hard look at the systems you use and how those systems contribute to or detract from effective collaboration between you.

The world of organisational systems is the one world where I see more people give up and believe that nothing can change than in any other area. The very people who have created the system then tell me it cannot change, even though they spend hours in meetings with others complaining about the impact it has on them. If we have not the time to really look at what we are doing and how it achieves what we want, then we continue to battle against ourselves.

Money matters

A critical question for organisations who want to enter into a Partnering relationship is to discuss openly and fully: 'How do we understand money?' If you do not have this conversation then you will find more unmanageable conflicts than profitable ones. I worked with two organisations that had formed a partnership to bid for the delivery of a major contract. This was a big job, big players, senior people. They had started out with the unspoken assumption that this was an equal partnership. They would share the costs of the bidding process. Meeting with them a year into the bidding process, I was fascinated to see the levels of dissent and unspoken conflicts in the group.

The reality was that one of the organisations stood to benefit considerably more from the job and had a different approach to the appropriate investment for a bid of this nature. The other organisation would lose some of its existing business should it not win the bid, so the stakes for its people were high. In addition, to minimise costs they had developed a lean culture, right down to always using public transport rather than taxis.

As a result, people in one organisation constantly felt like the poor relations. They would spend time sending verbal daggers across the room at the lack of tight financial controls. Then they'd go to yet another team lunch paid for by the other organisation every time. During the afternoon meetings there would be stabs at who never picked up the bill. This behaviour then moved into things like people arriving just in time for lunch, missing half the days agreed with no notice. All the usual passive aggressive behaviour that goes on when people are not managing their differences and the issues between them.

Now, don't get me wrong. I am not suggesting that these relationships have to be equal. Given their relative size and the potential rewards, it was appropriate in this instance for the two organisations to make different investments. It was just a shame that there had not been the useful conversation up front to understand how the different investments of time and resources would be understood and managed.

Money – how it is used, who has it, who takes their power from it and the meaning it is given – has to be understood when two organisations partner. Even more so for organisations who partner where one brings the money and the other does the work. Perhaps you have had similar conversations at home. We worked with an organisation which was committed to working in a Partnering way and whenever their senior leadership wanted to change the direction of the programme, would fall back to its position as the client and not consult the other 30 partners involved.

I believe that the difficult relationships between organisations in the West who fund work through Non-Governmental Organisations in other countries will not shift until they seriously start to talk about what it means to partner with a NGO in a different culture. And unless that conversation begins by understanding that money really does matter!

Getting it right from the start

Much of our focus in this chapter has been on Partnering with individuals and groups you already have a relationship with. Our final thoughts focus on some quick wins when establishing a new Partnering relationship. I have been called in to work with too many major projects that have overrun in terms of time and budget to discover that, had they just invested a small amount of time right in the beginning, many of the issues that plagued them would not have developed.

Holding onto Both-Gain

The negotiation phase is the place to start. The way in which you go about negotiating the project or programme lays the foundation for the future relationship and can present the issues that will plague you for the remainder of the programme.

We worked with a private sector organisation that had negotiated a construction deal in such a way that, near the end of the project, a large number of issues were raised in which the contractors were attempting to regain the losses they had incurred in securing the deal, which was won at a price no-one really believed was realistic. How do procurement teams understand their roles? Have you ever been in a tender process where the culture seems to be one of 'screwing the suppliers down, wringing them like wet flannels until their eyes water'? And then there seems to be some surprise that those smiling faces that were so sweet when they wooed us turned into slavering Rottweilers when the contract was signed.

This is also where the world of hidden agendas, hypotheses and unchecked assumptions run riot. Organisations have agendas, divisions have agendas as do teams and individuals. The sooner we stop demonising the notion of having agendas and assuming that they are hidden, the sooner our negotiations will move to Both-Gain.

Who are the people in your organisation who do the deals, negotiate the terms, navigate the financial straits? If we are committed to Partnering and fail to shift the way in which we measure the success of our deal-makers, then we will continue to pay the price during the contract.

No matter what the context, when people feel that there is an injustice it will not rest until there is some form of balance or, at worst, retribution.

How many times do you hear people say that their Partnering strategies are so effective they leave the contract in the bottom drawer?

As if it were failure to ever refer to it. So, what on earth are we spending so much time and resource on – setting up conflicts and disputes – for something we aspire to never using?

Champagne and canapés

We can accept the idea of having a party when the project's done and dusted, when we've struggled across the finishing line – even if the job is overdue or over budget. Perhaps we have sat nursing a warm glass of Chardonnay bitching about those bastards from the 'other side'? How about making the investment in spending some time together at the beginning, when there is time to plan for a great relationship, before it goes sour? How about having a Partnering launch? Invest the time and money to bring the key people who will be working together to establish their relationship and ways of working together. Give them time to discuss and agree on the assumptions that will guide the programme or project. Be creative in the way each organisation introduces itself to the other. What would a day in the life of someone in your organisation be like? How are decisions really taken, how do people navigate through the system? What are the conventions that you will agree on? Things like Project Management, Communication, Risk Management?

You will do well to spend a fair bit of time ensuring that everyone is very clear on what it is you are actually trying to do.

Safety nets

However well you plan, prepare and nurture a new Partnering relationship, one thing for sure is that there will still be some degree of conflict. We partner with people and that is what people do. And, as we considered in Chapter 5, that is great news because it gives us the essence of innovation. Particularly if we plan to work well with conflict. What are the things you are going to agree, up front, while the honeymoon is in full swing that will sustain the effective relationships between people?

Here are some things to think about.

Shall I mention a *Dispute Resolution Matrix?* I've managed to get you through a whole book without forcing my jargon onto you and now here's one of those phrases you love to hate. My assumption is that, by that phrase, you have a good idea what I'm going to say next, so I'm sticking with it.

Before the conflicts have begun, it is useful to think about the kinds of issues that may present differences and work out who and how this will be dealt with. The value of establishing this before the dispute arises is that you are more likely to be able to come up with a reasonable process before you are angry.

If many of the people on the project are working in a way that they rarely see each other or physically work together, you have got to bring them together regularly. I know this is something that is perceived wisdom – we all know it is better to be face to face. Do we, really? The simple truth is that, the longer people do not actually see each other, talk face to face, the easier it becomes to dehumanise them. It becomes more and more easy to assume hostile intent, to interpret their e-mails in a particular way. Most importantly, we tend not to raise challenging or difficult issues remotely. So, they build up because each time something happens we think we will wait till we see the person before raising it. By the time we meet up we have an entire rubbish dump of issues that have each built onto each other, resulting in a heap of assumptions fertilised into facts.

So, prepare to deal with conflict and make it work for you. Then, when you do cross the finish line, perhaps you are celebrating ahead of schedule and the party is a lavish one because you've invested your excess funds.

Whatever the context you find yourself in, the issues you face, the outcomes you are striving to achieve – there are ways in which you can achieve what you set out to – all it takes is to ensure that you have the right attitude – and get on with it!

A few final questions to affirmatively disrupt...

People and organisations go in the direction that we question them. Where will you go when you take some time to think about ...

What is the DNA of your organisation?

How are you contributing to the attitude and spirit of those around you?

What sort of world have you decided to notice?

Are notions of passion, possibility and potential part of the language that defines you?

What are your primary assumptions?

Which of the Partnering assumptions most challenge you?

What is the conflict you are allowing to plague you?

How long will you continue to be limited by fight or flight?

What direction are you determined to take people in?

If I asked your colleagues 'What was the most powerful question you have ever been asked?' How many of them would tell me about a conversation they had with you?

What will be different when you cash in on conflict?

The next book from Charlie Irvine focuses on…

making the most of

the chaos of human communication

by exploring the day-to-day use of the TICing model and sharpening the craft of questioning

What are you noTICing? What are you asking?

Charlie Irvine has come to see that what people notice and how they describe what they notice is greatly affected by the significant influences in their lives at that particular moment and the questions this prompts them to ask. To encourage people back to their senses, he relies on a handy prompt called the TICing model and the art of affirmative questioning – tools that help us stop in the middle of all the chaos and get curious not angry about the world around us.

If you're interested in success, getting curious is the first step in engaging with the world.

Get ready for Charlie Irvine's upcoming book on two crucial communication techniques. Using the TICing model, learn how to make sense of yourself and, surprisingly, other people. If you're curious enough about what could be different, get to understand the role of affirmative questioning and learn how and when to ask powerful questions.

The future you see before you will depend on it.

Printed in the United Kingdom
by Lightning Source UK Ltd.
112827UKS00001B/6